THE SWAMP FOX

Francis Marion's Campaign
in the Carolinas 1780

DAVID R. HIGGINS

First published in Great Britain in 2013 by Osprey Publishing
PO Box 883, Oxford, OX1 9PL, UK
PO Box 3985, New York, NY 10185-3985, USA
E-mail: info@ospreypublishing.com

Osprey Publishing is part of the Osprey Group

A CIP catalog record for this book is available from the British Library

Print ISBN: 978 1 78200 614 5
PDF ebook ISBN: 978 1 78200 615 2
ePub ebook ISBN: 978 1 78200 616 9

Index by Alan Rutter
Typeset in Sabon
Map by bounford.com
3D BEV by Donato Spedaliere
Originated by PDQ Media, Bungay, UK
Printed in China through Worldprint Ltd

13 14 15 16 17   10 9 8 7 6 5 4 3 2 1

Osprey Publishing is supporting the Woodland Trust, the UK's leading woodland conservation charity, by funding the dedication of trees.

www.ospreypublishing.com

AUTHOR'S ACKNOWLEDGMENTS

I would like to thank the following individuals for their kind support, without which this book, and my other military-history endeavors, might not have been possible: Chris Revels (Chief Ranger, Kings Mountain NMP), Ginny Fowler (Park Ranger, Cowpens National Battlefield), Carolyn Pilgrim (Berkeley County Museum), Alex Palkovich, Joseph Miranda, (editor-in-chief, *Modern War* magazine), Col (ret.) Jerry D. Morelock, PhD (editor-in-chief, *Armchair General* magazine), Nick Reynolds (commissioning editor, Osprey Publishing), the very helpful staff in the NARA microfilm, map, and photograph departments, and my wife, Diana.

Any errors or omissions in this work were certainly unintended, and for which I alone bear responsibility.

ARTIST'S NOTE

Readers may care to note that the original painting from which the cover of this book was prepared is available for private sale. All reproduction copyright whatsoever is retained by the Publishers. All inquiries should be addressed to:

mark@mrstacey.plus.com

The Publishers regret that they can enter into no correspondence upon this matter.

EDITOR'S NOTE

For ease of comparison please refer to the following conversion table:

1 mile = 1.6km
1yd = 0.9m
1ft = 0.3m
1in = 2.54cm/25.4mm
1 gallon (US) = 3.8 liters
1 ton (US) = 907kg
1lb = 0.45kg

CONTENTS

INTRODUCTION 4

ORIGINS 7

INITIAL STRATEGY 10
The rebellion comes to South Carolina 10
Britain's "Southern Strategy" 14
Charleston is threatened 16
A second revolution 18
Resistance is renewed 20
The battle of Camden 25

THE PLAN 27

THE RAID 34
Clash at Fishing Creek 36
Marion's raid on Nelson's Ferry 37
The British response 40
Skirmish at Kingstree 41
Skirmish at Blue Savannah 42
The British retaliate 48
Skirmish at Black Mingo 50
Marion's raid on Georgetown 53
Skirmish at Tearcoat Swamp 55
Richardson's Plantation to Ox Swamp 57
Skirmish at Allston's Plantation 59
Skirmish at Halfway Swamp 62
The battle of Cowpens 64
The "Bridges Campaign" 68
Final engagements 68

ANALYSIS 69

CONCLUSION 76

BIBLIOGRAPHY 78

INDEX 80

INTRODUCTION

For at least as long as large, conventional military forces have taken the field, irregular units have operated on the periphery, accomplishing those missions better suited to a less-regimented force. For conventional forces, the fact of being a state-supported or "legitimate" army, taking the field to conduct a "stand-up" fight against a similarly raised, armed, and organized adversary, merited a certain moral superiority. Such warfare was seen as having a semblance of rules, and limited the scope in which non-combatants were generally outside the purview of decisive battles of annihilation. Governmental forces further endeavored to use every instrument of national power to promote order and sustain their position. For them, maintaining security in an unstable environment required vast resources and incurred the handicap of frequently deviating from combat operations to achieve success.

When fighting from a place of weakness against such an adversary – whether it was numerically, technologically, or financially – options that were not as established or desirable were often all that was available to an insurgent or similar resistance movement bent on changing the political status quo. By definition, participants in such guerrilla wars tended to operate in distributed, less structured groups, which were often deemed less accepted or ethical because of the nature of their imposed methods of fighting. While the officers and men of such units were similarly held in poorer esteem than their conventional counterparts, they were often more reliable, mobile, and motivated when supplied with accurate intelligence, and certain of their cause. Strong leadership and individual initiative maximized movement, rapid combat tempos in the attack and defense, and a unit's ability to blend into the surrounding population or terrain. Experienced irregulars or partisans relied on being able to adapt rapidly to a variety of environments, climates, and situations to best ensure sustainment and ultimately survival. Limited in the amount of damage they could inflict on soft or inadequately defended enemy assets, including logistics or static, isolated outposts offered the choicest targets. They were also relatively free

to use every tool at their disposal to sow as much chaos and disorder as possible to achieve their goals. Although such tactics tended to amount to harassment if taken in isolation, the cumulative effect of such actions over enough time and space could wear significantly on a more established opponent's ability to operate.

As both sides attempted to outmaneuver or outlast the other and achieve ascendancy, winning over the population and gaining its acceptance as the legitimate governmental authority was paramount. To this end, government forces operated with the confidence that they were more or less invulnerable and actively sought a decisive battle with the guerrillas. When engaged in such a struggle, the design of the counterinsurgency campaign needed to reflect the population's cultural realities and social norms and conventions of war and peacemaking to communicate intent effectively. Should both sides effectively play to their strengths and fail to defeat the other, a stalemate could result. Although most combat, however violent and indiscriminate, relied on a modicum of accepted boundaries, such unresolved, festering conflicts frequently degenerated into a civil war, in which the social movements of neighbors and families frequently devolved into barbarity and terrorism. Even though such actions failed to serve a rational political objective or replace the parent social movement's ideology, participants often maintained an association with the larger effort.

With South Carolina largely consisting of undeveloped wilderness, waterways often facilitated movement better than the area's poorly maintained roads and trails. Boats, including flat-bottom varieties, such as those depicted here with Marion (mounted, second from left) on the Pee Dee River, proved to be valuable military assets. (Anne S.K. Brown Military Collection, Providence, RI, USA)

Intended to be placed atop an 11ft pedestal at a new veteran's memorial park at Venters Landing (aka Witherspoon's Ferry), Alex Palkovich's 10ft 6in-wide and 7ft-tall bronze sculpture depicts Francis Marion riding "Ball," named by Marion for its former Loyalist owner. (Courtesy of Alex Palkovich)

As the colonial possessions of Britain, France, and Spain pushed inland in the Americas during the 17th and 18th centuries, the large spaces and small populations meant irregular militias or similar bands were organized from the surrounding population to provide localized law and order or, in more established capacities, as supplementary forces for a conflict's duration. Typically these were directed against raids from native tribes that were being steadily pushed from their ancestral hunting grounds, foreign encroachment, or as protection against marauders. While in the relatively open European terrain British and French forces tended to rely on large, conventional armies and supplementary mercenaries, such forces were impractical in North America, which was a thinly populated country that produced little food, except along navigable rivers or where established land transport had been developed. In adapting to less formal tactics, much was based on light-infantry *Jäger* (huntsmen) formations that Prussia's King Frederick II instituted in the mid-1700s to perform duties such as infiltration, harassment, and reconnaissance.

With British and French forces possessing a legacy of large, permanent militaries, both tended to view American colonial military efforts with disdain, with one contemporary European observer stating that they were a "contemptible body of vagrants, deserters, and thieves." Many settlers had a relatively high standard of living and, and although most were willing to defend their property and homes, they generally lacked the incentive to fight beyond their respective militia's operational zones, or adhere to regimented military practices. Their frontier backgrounds, however, promoted firearms use, hunting, and horsemanship, which, in combination with experienced fighting natives, a mentality of self-sufficiency, and living in a largely wilderness environment, made colonial militia particularly adept at irregular warfare. As such, at the revolution's beginning in 1775, a British general prophetically wrote, "Our army will be destroyed by damn driblets… America is an ugly job… a damned affair indeed."

ORIGINS

As with any insurgency, the incubation stage of what became the American Revolution had festered for several years before the outbreak of open hostilities. Since the 1600s, maritime European nations had actively sought new colonies in the Americas, Africa, and Asia to stimulate their economies and increase their respective wealth. As these overseas possessions prospered via cheap natural resources such as gold, cotton, timber, tobacco, sugar cane, and furs, friction over determining their ownership, in addition to that of territory and trade, was common. As these resources were generally shipped to their respective home countries, converted into finished goods, and then resold to the colonists at inflated prices, Britain largely ignored its North American possessions. Amid the prevailing mercantilist, zero-sum mentality, in which European economic theory stressed that the more money one possessed, the less there was available for other – potentially rival – nations, exploitation was the result.

In order to manage the growing revenue streams better, Parliamentary bureaucracy and governmental intrusion and control increased accordingly. The Royal Navy began enforcing the old protectionist Navigation Acts, which were originally designed to keep foreign interests out of British colonial territories and now forced the colonists to export certain key goods. Parliament levied greater import duties and excise (sales) taxes on key items such as tobacco, sugar, beer, molasses, and tea, removed devalued paper currency, and ordered the colonists to quarter British forces as needed. Perhaps most egregious to the colonists, the Stamp Act (1765) imposed a tax for the use of such products as paper, legal documents, licenses, newspapers, and leaflets on penalty of vice-admiralty courts without a trial by jury.

While American colonists generally remained proud and loyal subjects, many found it increasingly clear that their king and Parliament thought of them not as their equals under the British constitution, but as inferiors to be exploited. More militant citizens viewed the Crown authority as a "foreign" presence intent on suppressing their liberty and questioned the conception of the empire in that, under the British constitution, a subject's property, in the form of taxes, could not be taken without their consent via domestic government representation. Americans seized upon Locke's "Second Treatise," in which he argued that, in extreme cases, when a ruler betrayed his people and the judges with the authority to hear their cause sided with the tyrant, the people could make an "Appeal to Heaven" when all other avenues had been exhausted. Such a concept provided a handy justification for the colonists' decision to resist imperial authority. After the Townshend Acts (1767), many colonists expanded on this premise, questioning whether Parliament had any legitimate jurisdiction over them at all – a mentality that fostered an emerging united national identity, although few advocated outright independence.

At the beginning of the American Revolutionary War, the relatively small British standing army was quickly expanded to fight in the colonies. Although this resulted in a high number of undesirables, the tough discipline and rigorous training of regular service made them, individually, among the world's best at contemporary, open-field combat. Their Continental adversaries generally lacked such qualities and, with supplemental colonial militias containing a high degree of low-quality fighters and opportunists,

THE FRENCH AND INDIAN WAR (1754–63)

As the last of four – essentially global – colonial conflicts, the French and Indian War (aka Seven Years War) pitted France (plus Austria and various native tribes) against Britain (plus Prussia, Hanover, and natives) across Europe, Central America, western Africa, India, the Philippines, and North America. While the war in Europe was largely a traditional stand-up fight, in the Americas irregular combat predominated in the sparsely populated wilderness, which promoted light, self-sustaining units. French army Regulars, however, never developed much capacity for irregular warfare, and preferred to retain a conventional mentality. This served to accelerate the downfall of the French, finally brought about by a greater British commitment, especially in the Thirteen Colonies, and the Royal Navy effectively severing its enemy's logistics at sea. By war's end as many as 1,400,000 people had died, but Great Britain emerged victorious, subsequently expelled its Bourbon rival, and took control of frequently disputed territory, including Rupert's Land (central Canada/Hudson Bay), New France (eastern Canada), Louisiana (eastern Louisiana to western New York), and Florida, having been ceded by Spain. The Native American tribes, however, were excluded from the peace settlement and unable to return to their former status after the resulting Pontiac's Rebellion.

By the end of the eight-year conflict, British national debt had skyrocketed from £72 million to over £122 million as the British government borrowed heavily from domestic and Dutch bankers; hundreds of thousands of this sum had been used to protect the American colonies. That year the British government, reasonably and legitimately from its point of view, moved to tighten the system of imperial control and to force the American colonists to contribute part of the £200,000 annual defense bill, which included the stationing of 10,000 soldiers along the frontier. In an attempt to rectify the situation, Parliament enacted a series of measures to increase tax revenue from its subjects, especially from the American colonies; a tall order considering the average annual amount royal customs collectors amassed that year was just £1,800. By this time, however, these territories had matured such that their interests and goals were increasingly distinct from those of the ruling classes in the mother country. Compounding the issue, the British monarch, George III, received all the profits from trade, passed laws limiting religion and freedom of movement, and refused to sanction a colonial standing army. Parliament frequently failed to understand or adjust to the situation and, with the French and much of the native threat eliminated, many colonists no longer needed or wanted further British "protection."

they could provide significant numbers of troops, but in units apt to dissolve in battle. As such, Washington refrained from training the provincials in irregular warfare techniques, and instead drilled them as a professional force. To accumulate and retain its strength, the Continental Army promised signing bonuses and land, and even forced or coerced those who had completed their three-month enlistments should they attempt to leave. Realizing early on that his command needed to fight predominantly on the defensive as a combat modifier, Washington attempted to contest the British and maintain the Continental Army in the field as a battlefield manifestation of colonial resistance.

Forced to maintain its legitimacy over the growing insurgency, the Continental Congress passed a boycott on British goods, which was enforced by the thousands of grassroots "committees of safety" across the colonies. Autonomous and with wide latitude, they emerged as "schools of revolution" that promoted local insurgents to enforce revolutionary discipline on their communities. Colonist-produced newspapers bypassed established varieties and enabled information to transfer across considerable distances, which helped build and unite a common political identity. In this manner, these extra-legal colonial institutions grew into the framework of an American government, which imparted legitimacy, and extended their authority to Congress. Without this infrastructure and supporting military, Congress would have never gained the level of power necessary to prosecute the war to any great degree. As it stood, they issued a "Declaration on the Causes and Necessity of Taking Up Arms" that detailed the colonists' reasons for fighting the British; it stated: "Honour, justice, and humanity, forbid us tamely to surrender that freedom which we received from our gallant ancestors" and that they were "with one mind, resolved to die freemen rather than live slaves."

THE FIRST CONTINENTAL CONGRESS

In response to increasing activist activity, especially around Boston, Massachusetts, Parliament implemented a series of punitive measures collectively known in America as the Intolerable (Coercive) Acts (1774). Outraged by the additional violations against their rights, colonial leaders organized the First Continental Congress (September 5 to October 26, 1774) in Philadelphia, Pennsylvania, to determine a unified course of action and to petition the king for a redress of grievances. With the situation around the city descending into rebellion, the port of Boston was subsequently closed and the Massachusetts governor, Major-General Sir Thomas Gage, was ordered to impose martial law over the colony. Cumulatively, such broad suppression tactics, including inciting native tribes to warfare, served to escalate tension. When 700 British soldiers moved on the village of Concord in April of 1775 with the intent of destroying a suspected colonist weapons depot, local minutemen militias drove them back to Boston. The Provincial Congress in Massachusetts responded by ordering 13,600 soldiers to be mobilized and colonial volunteers from across New England to converge on Boston to contest the British "occupation." The following month, the Second Continental Congress placed the colonies in a state of defense and unanimously voted in Major General George Washington to command a Continental Army.

INITIAL STRATEGY

The rebellion comes to South Carolina

Although the rebellion seemed to many to be a northern colonial issue, on June 18, 1775, the day after the first significant British/American fight at Bunker/Breed's Hill at Boston, the new royal governor, Lord William Campbell, arrived in Charleston (Charlestown or Charles-Town until its 1783 incorporation), South Carolina, with an unaccustomedly small degree of pomp. Known as the "London of the Lowcountry," the city had a mostly English and Barbadian (Barbados) population of some 12,000 (180,000 in the entire colony, which was dwarfed by the mother country's 10 million). For the colony it was an important port, which, to a lesser degree with Georgetown and Beaufort/Port Royal Island, had profited greatly from natural resource exploitation and slave labor. As such, by the mid-1770s the Lower South's population was just 59 percent white, compared with the 79 percent colonial average, with only two-thirds of the white population having English ancestry.

In concert with their northern compatriots, after removing most royal officials and their Loyalist (Tory) supporters from positions of authority, the Whigs (those supporting independence) established a Provincial Congress on July 6, 1774, which then sent five elected delegates to the First Continental Congress in Philadelphia. On December 19, parish elections had been held to choose delegates for the First Provincial Congress in Charleston on January 11, 1775 to undertake the governing of the colony. Local committees were then established under an Executive Council of Safety to enforce regulations. In addition to adopting the American Bill of Rights and the Act of Association, by which the colonies would not import British goods, the South Carolina Provincial Congress sent a delegation asking that the new governor help dissuade George III from his view of the colony's disloyalty. Campbell, however, had lobbied hard to secure his new position, which in reality was to bring the region's growing civil unrest to heel, and remained steadfast in his recognition of Britain being the region's sole authority. Focusing on the mass printing of pamphlets to undermine the unauthorized government and exploit the political and socioeconomic rift between the area's low country aristocracy and the commoners farther inland, growing rebel violence and intimidation eventually forced him from Charleston after only three months of service.

Having struggled to carve a living from the wilderness, which involved contesting raids by Native Americans and bandits, vigilante groups were formed to provide a degree of legal authority in the backcountry. To counter the crude, often excessive actions of these "Regulators," which included resisting Crown taxation and authority, "Counter-regulators" similarly degenerated to being little more than retaliatory gangs. Amid such an acrimonious environment, some simply avoided the fray as best they could. Others signed up with militias, either for protection or to seek retribution or plunder, often with little mind to the group's political leaning, as long as it seemed successful or dominant. In the Lower South (Georgia and the Carolinas) such guerrilla activity occurred as early as July of 1775, when bands like Joseph Habersham's "Liberty Boys" undertook minor mounted raids and harassment against British and Loyalist authority and, incidentally, neutrals, around Savannah, Georgia. Others, such as Moore's Creek Bridge

A reconstruction of the appearance of a typical South Carolina militiaman wearing a woolen hunting frock with fringe, homemade linen/cotton blouse, white linen body shirt, felt hat, belly cartridge box, belt frog, haversack, and brown-dyed, full wool gaiters for protection when walking through underbrush (note the cottonmouth snake at his feet). (Author, courtesy of the Berkeley Museum)

(February 27, 1776), near Wilmington, North Carolina, were more traditional battles, which in this example essentially secured the colony for the rebels. While Loyalist sentiment extended throughout the south, many of the region's coastal residents remained neutral or sympathized with the rebellion. Inland, significant opposition to the Crown came from Irish, Scottish, and Huguenot immigrants, who, as a result of the Township Act of 1730, had left Europe for a variety of political, religious, or financial interests, and maintained an ancestral dislike for all things British.

In response to the unfolding conflict centered in Massachusetts, the South Carolina Provisional Congress voted to raise the 1st and 2nd South Carolina (infantry) and 3rd "Ranger" (cavalry) regiments of 500 men each. Able to integrate with the Continental Army if needed, they were commonly led by those who had held royal commissions and reneged on their sworn allegiance to the king. Based on votes for command and seniority, Lieutenant-Colonel William Moultrie, a veteran of the Anglo-Cherokee War (1758–61), was to command the 2nd South Carolina Regiment. His rather reluctant subordinate, Francis Marion, was made one of ten regimental captains on June 17, 1775, and sent into the Santee, Black, and Pee Dee River areas to organize rebel sympathizers from a backwoods population that were spoiling for a fight.

FRANCIS MARION

Slight to the point of frailty, with black, piercing eyes, high forehead, jutting jaw, and aquiline nose, Francis Marion (1732 to February 27, 1795) appeared the antithesis of the stereotypical partisan commander. Descended from Huguenots (Calvinist Protestants), his grandparents had fled religious persecution in Catholic France in 1690 to start a new, generally hard farming life along the Santee River. The last of six children, Marion suffered with ankles and knees that were slightly deformed at birth, and he was so sickly and small that, in addition to his parents having been unsure he would live, his friend, Peter Horry, later commented, "he had it on good authority that this great soldier at his birth, was no larger than a New England lobster, and might easily enough have been put into a quart pot."

Having had an apparently normal childhood, replete with French language and customs, Marion, along with his siblings, received a basic education. At age 15, his parents granted permission for him to serve on a six-man schooner out of Georgetown, believing the physically demanding experience would have beneficial effects upon their son's small stature. On returning from the West Indies, however, the boat was struck and sunk by a whale and, after making landfall after five days on a lifeboat, Marion decided to return to farming rice and indigo; his health seemingly improved. In 1756 he joined the Upper St John's militia under Captain John Postell, and later served as a first lieutenant under his friend, Captain William Moultrie, to contest a renewed Cherokee border uprising, a response to white settlers encroaching upon their ancestral hunting grounds along the colony's expanding western border. Marion exhibited an aptitude for conducting irregular combat, his superior remarking that he "was an active, brave, and hardy soldier, and an excellent partisan officer."

During the subsequent decade Marion toiled at his lucrative farm, and in 1773 was able to purchase "Pond Bluff," a mansion on the Santee near Eutaw Springs. Following the South Carolina Whigs electing their first Provincial Congress, St John's Parish chose him to co-represent them along with his brother in Charleston. While Marion was serving, word arrived of the Massachusetts militia in Lexington firing on British Regulars from Boston, to which the delegates pledged themselves to stand united in the defense of South Carolina.

A depiction of Francis Marion; no known created-from-sight portrait of him exists. In the rugged environments in which Marion operated, such an official-looking uniform was likely not worn, and instead his attire would have been a mix of items incorporating his 2nd South Carolina uniform and civilian dress. (Harper & Brothers, 1852)

During the war, Marion participated in the siege of Savannah in 1779, and gained a reputation for being able to instill discipline, order, and tidiness – as well as devotion – in his men. Generally kind, he could be short, overly sensitive, and resentful of taking orders from peers, especially during one of his "dark moods." To maintain hygiene in the field, he strictly enforced his men having short, combed hair, and – as was customary for English-speaking men of the period – no facial hair. Marion also had little tolerance for disobedience, plundering, and alcohol consumption, made evident on January 29, 1781, when he ordered Captain John Postell from the Kingstree Regiment – his former commander – to "Take care that your men do not get at liquor, or clog themselves with plunder so as to endanger their retreat."

In conducting a guerrilla campaign, Francis Marion was well suited to the task, in that he, and the majority of his followers, had experience in operating in a wilderness environment. As most rebel and Loyalist ranks comprised farmers, or had jobs related to farming, whose families had scratched a living in the swampy, rugged South Carolina lowlands, they also possessed supplementary hunting skills, including shooting, tracking, stealth, self-sufficiency, and survival.

After some three months of training and drill, the new South Carolina units were ready for activation, but, with no official flag, the Council of Safety delegated Moultrie to create one. As his men wore silver crescents and black plumes on their hats, he decided on a blue banner, with a silver crescent in the upper corner, which was soon raised defiantly over Fort Johnson on Charleston Harbor's south coast. Three months later, Moultrie secured the opposite side of the haven's entrance at Sullivan Island, and ordered his men to wear blue coats with scarlet linings, facings, and cuffs, and white buttons, waistcoats, and breeches to differentiate their dress from the predominantly red uniform of the British.

The adoption of a constitution by the South Carolina Provincial Congress on March 26, 1776, with John Rutledge elected as president, and the 2nd South Carolina Regiment's success in driving off a Royal Navy amphibious invasion of Charleston at Fort Sullivan on June 28, 1776, combined to promote the spread of rebellious fervor throughout South Carolina and helped to validate the independence proclaimed in Philadelphia. With the British threat removed for the foreseeable future, in celebration Susannah Elliott, the wife of an officer from the recently formed 4th South Carolina Regiment, presented Moultrie's command with a pair of silk flags – one red and the other blue. Both were richly embroidered with "IID:REGT" in yellow, with a green wreath and a red ribbon surrounding "Vita Potior Libertas" ("Liberty rather than life"). The new government established its authority, in part by adopting loyalty measures designed to elicit Loyalist support on threat of banishment from the colony. While such purging measures brought a degree of stability, they masked an increasing resentment and hostility among those remaining loyal to the Crown, as they were forced to maintain a low profile, fight, or relocate to Loyalist refuges, such as Florida, Georgia, or Canada.

JUNE 28, 1776

Battle of Fort Sullivan

Originally a rebel-constructed series of defenses built in 1776 to protect the entrance to Charleston Harbor (background), Fort Sullivan's Palmetto log embrasures proved surprisingly resilient when hit by cannon fire. After contributing to the successful repulse of a British amphibious attack on June 28, 1776, the structure was progressively modernized as Fort Moultrie until decommissioned in 1947. (Author)

Having arrived at Washington's winter encampment at Valley Forge on February 23, 1778, the unemployed Prussian officer, Baron von Steuben, was tasked with drilling the largely inexperienced American Continentals in contemporary military practices. (NARA)

Britain's "Southern Strategy"

Although the British won a majority of the battles and skirmishes throughout Canada, New York, New Jersey, and Rhode Island over the first two years of the conflict, Washington's sometimes draconian handling of the Continental Army, and Prussian drill-master Baron Friedrich von Steuben's effective training, helped it remain in the field, and thereby kept the rebellion alive. By March of 1778, George III was eager to resolve what had become a political and military quagmire, and put forth the Carlisle Peace Commission in a guarded attempt to cease hostilities, but American insistence that Britain first recognize colonial independence spelled its failure. Faced with an intractable problem, British Prime Minister, Lord Frederick North, and the Secretary of State for the American Department, Lord George Germain (the official directly responsible to Parliament for the nation's handling of the war), came under intense political pressure to achieve a military victory. As dispatches could take several months to travel across the Atlantic Ocean, the latter toiled to develop a strategy that could be implemented by the largely autonomous commander in-theater.

On March 8, 1778, Germain sent a letter to Howe's replacement, Lieutenant-General Henry Clinton, declaring that conquering the southern states of Georgia, South Carolina, and North Carolina was absolutely essential, and that this was "considered by the King as an object of great importance in the scale of the war." The best way to accomplish this was simply to cut off the more actively rebellious colonies by securing the Lower South and Virginia. As the American government used the revenue generated by exporting crops such as rice, indigo, and tobacco to purchase war stocks and equipment from Europe, the move would also theoretically cripple the rebels' economic base. To assure success most effectively, Germain gave Clinton broad latitude in planning the invasion of the south. As an American delegation had recently secured French help in the form of soldiers, ships, and supplies, a rapid British counterstroke was to concentrate on

the southern colonies where, it was believed, numerous Loyalists awaited the necessary encouragement to recover control of the Lower South, as the presence of either British or American Regular forces tended to encourage the turnout of their respective militias, often significantly.

Although Britain's first military foray into the south had ended in failure two years earlier at Sullivan Island, Parliament remained convinced of the validity of a renewed campaign. With the war in the north having reached a stalemate following the American victory at Second Saratoga (October 7, 1777) and a draw at Monmouth Courthouse (June 28, 1778), on December 19, 1779 the British readied to enact their southern campaign and a renewed attempt to take Charleston. The following month, Clinton sent a British fleet with some 9,000 soldiers from New York toward Charleston; it was to join a command raised by Major General Augustine Prévost from the Florida garrison at St Augustine. Although Clinton had initially resisted such an endeavor, he now hoped to impose a strategy of attrition by seizing a series of coastal towns, which would force Washington to disperse his forces and commensurately reduce pressure upon the British in the north. With Spain having declared war on England on June 16, 1779 – even though the Spanish did not make an alliance with the American Revolutionary forces – and Congress having approved a peace plan that stipulated independence, a complete British evacuation of America, and free navigation on the Mississippi River, Crown forces needed to achieve victory in the south before foreign intervention became a serious threat.

Typical of the swampy terrain along the Santee River, this view near Fort Watson shows cypress, southern live oak, and sweetgum. This terrain restricted movement to the region's few roads or navigable waterways, and housed a variety of fauna including alligators and vipers. (Author)

MARCH 29 TO
MAY 12, 1780

Siege of Charleston

Charleston is threatened

Although Moultrie (now a major general) defeated a British detachment at Port Royal Island in early 1780, the enemy had pressed ahead, scoring victories at Augusta (occupied January 31, 1779), Brier Creek (March 3, 1779), and elsewhere. Over the next few months, Crown and Loyalist forces gained control over Georgia and threatened Charleston. Having failed to dislodge the enemy from Savannah, which had fallen to British forces in December of 1778, the American Southern Department commander, Major General Benjamin Lincoln, called for reinforcements to counter the threat on the area; few materialized. On February 11, 1780, British troops arrived at Simmons Island, 20 miles southwest of Charleston, after a difficult sea journey, and began their steady operation to isolate and eliminate the town's defenders, as its defenses were deemed too formidable for a direct assault. Although military prudence dictated abandoning the area, municipal leaders pressured Lincoln to remain. As the 10,000-strong British army compromised Charleston's defenses, the fatalistic mood of those caught within the perimeter translated into numerous parties to "celebrate" their final days of freedom.

On March 19, Marion (a lieutenant colonel commandant – a title granting superiority over those with the base rank – since September 16, 1776) attended one such dinner hosted by Moultrie's adjutant general, Captain Alexander McQueen. As was custom, the host soon locked all the first-floor doors and windows, so the guests could not "escape" until all the alcohol had been consumed. Never a drinker (he apparently enjoyed a mix of water and vinegar), Marion attempted to leave by jumping from a second-story window, whereupon he fractured his ankle and was deemed unfit for duty. Subsequently evacuated from the city to along the Santee River, Marion found that his status as the 2nd South Carolina commander made him a known personality, and one the numerous British patrols looked to capture. As such, for the next several months, Marion was covertly shuffled among various locations owned by rebel sympathizers.

The siege of Charleston began on March 29. On April 8, Clinton summoned Lincoln to surrender, but, with the latter responding that he was determined to fight to the last, the British initiated a bombardment of the besieged town. With Lincoln having convinced Rutledge (now governor) to leave Charleston in order to "keep alive the civil authority," the possibility of extricating some of the defenders to potentially fight the British on

"Plan of the Siege of Charleston in South Carolina" (March 29–May 12, 1780) depicts British and American positions before the city, Fort Sullivan (upper right), and Royal Navy ships near Fort Johnson (right). Once the British cut off the peninsula's neck, the resulting American predicament was obvious. (Stedman's *History of the Origin, Progress, and Termination of the American War*)

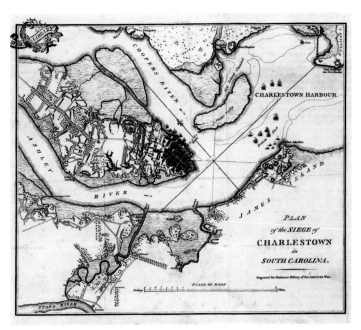

better terms became unfeasible, as city leaders threatened to let the British enter unopposed should such action be undertaken. With Charleston's defenses increasingly untenable, Lincoln presented two conditional surrender terms, but Clinton would accept nothing short of an unconditional solution. Forced to agree to the British ultimatum, the American defenders surrendered on May 12, having suffered 89 killed, 138 wounded, and 3,371 captured. For 99 dead and 217 wounded, the British captured 311 artillery pieces, 5,916 muskets, and thousands of rounds of ammunition. Although surrendering officers were generally exchanged or paroled, a common practice to avoid having to feed and house such captives, the lower ranks were sent to nearby prison ships where 45 percent would die in captivity. In British hands, Charleston would serve as a primary base from which to receive supplies and replacements as they advanced inland; for their adversaries, the city's capture made it nearly untenable to maintain a presence in South Carolina, after what amounted to the single largest surrender of American forces until the battle of Corregidor in 1942.

In response to the deteriorating rebel presence in the Lower South, Washington's Continental Army in the north was in little position to assist directly, being severely reduced in numbers and ill supported by Congress. Relying on militia and rebel sympathizers to protect the northern colonies,

This print illustrates the enclosed, disease-ridden conditions common aboard prison ships during the Revolutionary War. The ship depicted here is HMS *Jersey* off Long Island, but those in Charleston Harbor would have been much the same. (NARA)

Opposite:
Area of operations of
Francis Marion and Banastre
Tarleton in the Carolinas,
1776–83.

To assist friend-or-foe
identification on the
smoke-obscured battlefields
of the period, the British
first adopted red uniforms in
1645. The "RP" and crown
on the buttons here indicate
"Royal Provincials." At Kings
Mountain (October 7, 1780),
those Loyalists serving in the
British Army were the only
units to wear this uniform.
(Author, courtesy of Kings
Mountain NPS)

Washington released nearly 2,000 men from the Maryland division and Delaware militia to defend the Carolinas – a sizeable number, considering his command comprised just 10,500 soldiers, 2,800 of whom were to be discharged in April of 1780. Under Johann von Robais, Baron de Kalb, the force soon left Morristown, New Jersey, with their wives, children, and various camp followers in tow. De Kalb had hoped to be reinforced by Continental authorities en route, but received little help, meaning those without wagons or horses had to carry their own arms, equipment, and food.

De Kalb understood the need to draw upon and organize the thousands of militiamen roaming the South Carolina countryside under Brigadier General Thomas Sumter and North Carolinian Major General Richard Caswell. De Kalb received word of Charleston's capitulation while still in Virginia, but continued south, crossing into North Carolina on June 20. As many British senior commanders viewed these militiamen as stragglers from Crown service, harsh efforts were commonly used to bring them to heel, as reflected by the Camden District militia commander, Major Henry Rugeley, who stated, "I will give the inhabitants ten guineas for the head of any deserter belonging to the volunteers of Ireland, and five guineas only if they bring him in alive." As the only senior regimental or Continental officer to escape capture at Charleston, Marion rode for North Carolina alongside his friend and comrade-in-arms, Major Peter Horry, contacting de Kalb's command at Coxe's Mill as soon as they were able in early July.

A second revolution

Following Charleston's fall, and overruling Washington's desire to appoint Brigadier General Nathanael Greene to the post, Congress replaced Lincoln with Brigadier General Horatio Gates as Southern Department commander on June 13, 1780 – in part because Congress believed that southern militiamen would rally to him as their northern compatriots had done following Gates' proclaimed victory at Second Saratoga in October of 1777. Born in England and having entered British Army service as a boy, Gates had served with Washington during the French and Indian War before retiring. At the Revolutionary War's start, the need for experienced commanders in the fledgling Continental Army resulted in Gates' reinstatement as a brigadier general; his administrative skill would be overshadowed by his suspect abilities as a battlefield leader.

Believing the Carolinas subdued, before leaving for New York, Clinton had ordered Lieutenant-General Charles Cornwallis to raise Loyalist militias to help pacify the sparsely populated, largely wilderness interior of Georgia and the Carolinas. Under Major Patrick Ferguson, young men with fewer than three children were to serve for six months, while those aged over 40 or with larger families were to form a "domestick militia" responsible for maintaining local order. They were

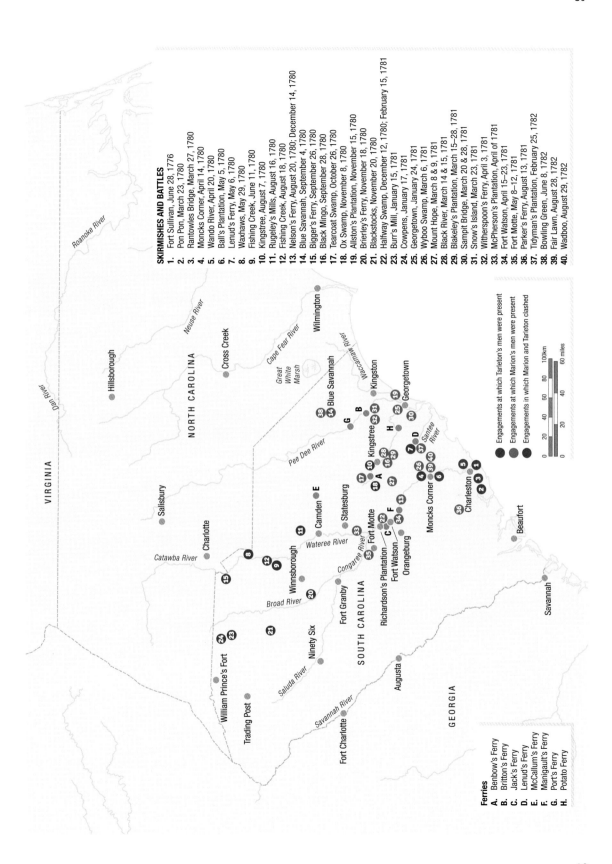

SKIRMISHES AND BATTLES

1. Fort Sullivan, June 28, 1776
2. Pon Pon, March 23, 1780
3. Rantowles Bridge, March 27, 1780
4. Moncks Corner, April 14, 1780
5. Wando River, April 20, 1780
6. Ball's Plantation, May 5, 1780
7. Lenud's Ferry, May 6, 1780
8. Waxhaws, May 29, 1780
9. Fishing Creek, June 11, 1780
10. Kingstree, August 7, 1780
11. Rugeley's Mills, August 16, 1780
12. Fishing Creek, August 18, 1780
13. Nelson's Ferry, August 20, 1780; December 14, 1780
14. Blue Savannah, September 4, 1780
15. Bigger's Ferry, September 26, 1780
16. Black Mingo, September 28, 1780
17. Tearcoat Swamp, October 26, 1780
18. Ox Swamp, November 8, 1780
19. Allston's Plantation, November 15, 1780
20. Brierley's Ferry, November 18, 1780
21. Blackstocks, November 20, 1780
22. Halfway Swamp, December 12, 1780; February 15, 1781
23. Burr's Mill, January 15, 1781
24. Cowpens, January 17, 1781
25. Georgetown, January 24, 1781
26. Wyboo Swamp, March 6, 1781
27. Mount Hope, March 8 & 9, 1781
28. Black River, March 14 & 15, 1781
29. Blakeley's Plantation, March 15–28, 1781
30. Sampit Bridge, March 20 & 28, 1781
31. Snow's Island, March 23, 1781
32. Witherspoon's Ferry, April 3, 1781
33. McPherson's Plantation, April of 1781
34. Fort Watson, April 15–23, 1781
35. Fort Motte, May 8–12, 1781
36. Parker's Ferry, August 13, 1781
37. Tidyman's Plantation, February 25, 1782
38. Bowling Green, June 8, 1782
39. Fair Lawn, August 28, 1782
40. Wadboo, August 29, 1782

Ferries

A. Benbow's Ferry
B. Britton's Ferry
C. Jack's Ferry
D. Lenud's Ferry
E. McCallum's Ferry
F. Manigault's Ferry
G. Port's Ferry
H. Potato Ferry

Engagements at which Tarleton's men were present
Engagements at which Marion's men were present
Engagements in which Marion and Tarleton clashed

0   20   40   60   80   100km
0   20   40   60 miles

19

to be respectively organized into companies and battalions under an elected member, where they were armed and paid as per army rates, and were officially prohibited from harassing peaceful civilians. Clinton also called for those holding "public station" or militia field commissions under the rebel government to be sent to one of the coastal islands as "prisoners of war on parole." Violent offenders were to be imprisoned, while those that remained peaceful were to be simply disarmed and made to "furnish moderate contributions of provisions, waggons [sic], horses, etc."

Cornwallis had already established a series of forts along the coast and interior rivers to consolidate his hold on Georgia and South Carolina: Savannah and Augusta (Savannah), Charleston, Beaufort, Ninety Six and Granby (Saluda), Orangeburg (Edisto), Motte (Congaree/Wateree), and Watson (Santee). Of these, Camden's location between the coast and Cornwallis's next goal, North Carolina, made it a key possession; it also maintained communication with Ninety Six via a small post at Rocky Mount. Believing that should such a move fail, "we must give up both South Carolina & Georgia and retire within the walls of Charlestown," Cornwallis decided to secure Charlotte, essentially a crossroads with some 20 homes and a courthouse, before striking east to Cross Creek (present-day Fayetteville) and the Cape Fear River.

Apparently Clinton foresaw Cornwallis advancing north along the Carolina coast in conjunction with the Royal Navy, developing Loyalist bases, then moving inland: a seemingly methodical but progressive campaign to consolidate the colony before moving on Virginia. As the theater commander lacked money, horses, wagons, and food to carry out the orders, and also was not politically secure, Cornwallis initially applied a softer touch promoted by his superior, confiscating absentee rebel property, returning that stolen from Loyalists, and applying a generous parole policy. By June, however, his attitude began to change on learning that many of the enemy being encountered had reneged on their paroles, as word of Gates' approaching army spread. Within a month, it became obvious that the rebel cause in South Carolina had not been eliminated; Cornwallis complained that, in addition to a lack of discipline and resolve among many Loyalist militias, "the whole country" between the Pee Dee and Santee rivers was "… in an absolute state of rebellion, every friend of the government had been carried off, and his plantation destroyed."

Resistance is renewed

On July 25, 1780 Gates arrived in Coxe's Mill, North Carolina, to take command of a reconstituted "grand army" of predominantly Virginia and North Carolina militia. With the remaining rebel resistance in South Carolina offered by predominantly untested partisan companies, such as those commanded by Andrew Pickens (west), Thomas Sumter (center), and Francis Marion (east), the new Southern Department commander met with many of these leaders best to orchestrate an offensive with his Continentals. With his new command suffering from malnutrition, the American commander looked to boost morale by marching for British-held Camden, with the

As part of the network of British outposts in South Carolina, Fort Motte's placement along the Congaree River helped maintain logistics and communications along the Santee River to Georgetown. (Benson J. Lossing, 1850)

intention of defeating Lieutenant-Colonel Francis Rawdon, the British commander at Camden, hopefully with help from the district's predominantly Scottish, Irish, and Quaker residents.

Though Gates' subordinates approved of his decision, they recommended first moving through Charlotte and Salisbury to obtain food, fresh water, and supplies from the area's largely Presbyterian rebel sympathizers. This area was one in which Rawdon had recently burned a number of churches, as Calvinist institutions were believed to preach sedition, seemingly evidenced by their emphasis on congregational voting and democratically elected ministers. Against the majority council, and without knowing the full capabilities of his new command, Gates made directly for Camden, located in a region known for its strong Loyalist sympathies, where his force was expected to scavenge. Confident of victory, Gates neglected to attack his enemy's communications, believing he would repeat his 1777 success, even though the tactical defensive victory at Saratoga was against an inexperienced and overconfident British commander, Major-General John Burgoyne.

Gates set out for Camden on July 27, intent on establishing a defensive position to entice the British to attack him. Having crossed the Pee Dee River a week later, the American army continued to push Rawdon's roughly 1,000 British Regulars and militia back on his base at Camden. On August 4, Marion and his small, ragged band of "burlesque" irregulars, with their black leather caps, rode into Gates' camp, much to the mirth of many in the reconstituted southern army who were accustomed to a more military bearing. Still nursing his "very crazy" ankle, their commander was subsequently incorporated into Gates' staff, where he received regular intelligence reports from his partisan subordinates.

The Santee River (shown here between Murphy's Ferry and Lenud's Ferry) was a key waterway, as it meandered some 143 miles from Singleton's Mill to reach the coast between Georgetown and Charleston. Its watershed includes the Wateree, Broad, and Saluda rivers. (Author)

Having been instrumental in helping the British to encircle Charleston, Lieutenant-Colonel Banastre Tarleton's dragoons crossed the Santee River at Lenud's Ferry en route to Camden and passed into Williamsburg District to investigate rumors of a 500-man rebel force under Major John James at Indiantown. Aware of the enemy cavalry's approach, Captain William McCottry rode off with his command to counter it, but his adversary had been similarly apprised of the developing situation by Loyalists on August 6/7 at Kingstree's Black River Bridge around midnight. Unwilling to contest a numerically superior force in the dark, Tarleton withdrew, but not before burning the house of Marion's first cousin and closest friend, Captain Henry Mouzon. When Major James learned of Tarleton's raid into the predominantly Scottish, Irish, and Huguenot Williamsburg District, he sent his now homeless compatriot to ask Gates to send an experienced commander.

With the British having had a presence in nearby Georgetown since capturing it without a fight on July 1, in his capacity as opposition leader Major James had gone to the new garrison commander, Captain John P. Ardesoif of the Royal Navy, to ask what was expected of the people in Williamsburg. Having previously invited the surrounding inhabitants to swear allegiance to the Crown and accept its protection, Ardesoif was irritated that many remained defiant. Presented with an ultimatum that included the

BANASTRE TARLETON

Born into a merchant family, with considerable ties to the British American colonies, Banastre Tarleton (August 21, 1754 to January 15, 1833) received an education from Oxford University as preparation for a career as a lawyer. Although his father's death in 1773 provided him with a £5,000 inheritance, he soon gambled most of it away, but managed to retain enough to purchase a commission as a cornet (second lieutenant) in the British Army's 1st Dragoon Guards. As an officer, his skills in horsemanship and leadership garnered the attention of his superiors, resulting in steady promotions. In December of 1775, he sailed with Cornwallis for Charleston, South Carolina, but,

failing to pass rebel-held Fort Sullivan, the fleet moved instead for New York. Having proven himself as a bold, creative field commander, Tarleton was given command of the British Legion, a mixed horse and light-infantry formation, from which he gained his greatest success and notoriety. Having conducted a largely successful campaign throughout much of South Carolina in 1780, Tarleton's defeat at Cowpens saw his – and British – fortunes decline, ending with his capture and parole at Yorktown, Virginia, the next year. Following his subsequent return to England, he entered politics and, by 1812, had risen to full general.

words "though you have rebelled against his majesty he offers you a free pardon of which you were undeserving, for you ought all to have been hanged," Major James responded that those he represented would refuse such conditions. Irate at his guest using the word "represent," an angry Ardesoif replied, "You damned rebel! If you speak in such language, I will immediately order you to be hanged up to the yard arm." Having anticipated the conversation's threatening direction, James thrust his chair into the captain's face, slipped out of the house's back door, and rode off for Kingstree on his mount, Thunder.

On receiving Major James' new information, a meeting of Williamsburg District inhabitants produced a unanimous decision to fight, and word was quickly passed to the surrounding area. Within two days, the Kingstree Regiment's four companies – each roughly 50 strong and led by captains John James Jr, John McCauley, and Robert and William McCottry – formed up in Williamsburg District. Colonel Hugh Giles soon arrived with companies under captains Robert Thornley and James Witherspoon, with Major James elected to command the entire force, having had the most experience in such a capacity and being their legislative representative.

As Rawdon steadily withdrew southward, on August 8 Tarleton's mounted contingent arrived, having ravaged the Black River area in order to punish its rebel inhabitants. Having commanded British forces at Waxhans the previous May – in which his legion had overwhelmed a larger force of Virginian Continentals led by Colonel Abraham Buford and heading for North Carolina – and subsequently bayoneted more than 100 Continentals

Having fought in the Revolutionary War since December of 1775, Banastre Tarleton gained a reputation as an innovative, aggressive dragoon commander, which was tempered by battlefield excesses that were often exaggerated and propagandized by the rebels – especially during the southern campaign while he served under Cornwallis. (Harper & Brothers, 1852)

2nd BRIGADE OF SOUTH CAROLINA MILITIA, AUGUST 16, 1780

Commander: Lieutenant Colonel Francis Marion
Second in command: Lieutenant Colonel Hugh Ervin
Beaufort District Regiment (Lieutenant Colonel Edward Barnwell)
Charles Town (Charleston) District Regiment (Colonel Alexander Moultrie)
Cheraws District Regiment (Colonel Abel Kolb)
Georgetown District (aka Britton's Neck) Regiment (Colonel John Ervin)
Berkeley County Regiment (Colonel Richard Richardson Jr)
Upper Craven County (aka Pee Dee) Regiment (Colonel Jacob Baxter)

Lower Craven County (aka Lynches River) Regiment (Colonel Hugh Giles)
Colleton County Regiment (Colonel John Sanders)
Upper Granville County Regiment (Lieutenant Colonel William Harden)
Lower Granville County Regiment (Lieutenant Colonel William Stafford)
Kingstree (aka Williamsburg Township) Regiment (Colonel Archibald McDonald)
Kershaw Regiment (Colonel John Marshall)
Maham's Light Dragoons (Lieutenant Colonel Hezekiah Maham)

While commanding the American right flank at Camden (August 16, 1780), Baron de Kalb was mortally wounded, and his overwhelmed Maryland and Delaware Continentals were finally forced to follow Gates' routed army. (Anne S.K. Brown Military Collection, Providence, RI, USA)

who attempted to surrender amid the chaos of combat, the dragoon commander had garnered a dubious reputation. As exaggerations or distortions of such actions were frequently used by both sides in their propaganda, this debated incident was soon spun as indicative of British treatment and subsequently used as a rebel rallying cry: "Buford's Massacre" or "Tarleton Quarter."

Alerted to Gates' movement on August 9, Cornwallis set out the next evening from Charleston for Camden, arriving four days later; this increased British forces to 2,239 soldiers fit for duty. Had his American adversary pushed on at this time, he could well have exploited Rawdon's flank and taken the prized town. Instead, he remained idle for two days, and arrived at Rugeley's Mill, some 12 miles north of his goal, only on August 13, by which time the British commander had received reinforcements and erected redoubts to protect his position at the town. Although Gates had a paper strength of some 4,100 men, exhaustion and heatstroke from marching, and high temperatures, limited fresh water, and having subsisted, in part, on unripened green corn that caused dysentery, just 3,052 were on hand – a typical figure, as such ailments, including fevers, typhus, "fluxes," and what was believed at the time to be "mysterious effluvia or miasma rising from the swamps," commonly removed one in every five combatants, especially in the south.

Having been informed of Cornwallis's movements toward Camden only on August 14, Gates was happy to release Marion to command the Williamsburg District militia, likely just to be rid of the "burlesque" distraction Marion's followers presented in camp. Tasked with orders to destroy all the boats along the lower Santee River to prevent Cornwallis from escaping, to provide intelligence, and to inform the citizenry of the American commander's intent to protect them from "acts of barbarity and devastation," the new partisan commander left Rugeley's Mill on August 15.

The battle of Camden

With Tarleton's 250 dragoons having provided intelligence of the surrounding area on August 15, including the enemy army's proximity from three captured American pickets, Cornwallis set out north from Camden at 10.00pm, with the intention of striking his adversary on the march. As the British quietly marched through the darkness, a skirmish of pickets commenced at around 2.30am on August 16, which forced a halt along a narrow strip of land bordered by swampy terrain. With the threat of being flanked essentially eliminated by the terrain, the British commander felt confident that his numerically inferior force could defend its position. By dawn, Cornwallis had deployed his army into two ranks, with his veteran Regulars on the right under Lieutenant-Colonel James Webster. Rawdon's Irish volunteers occupied the opposite flank, with Loyalists between them. The 63rd Regiment of Foot stood in reserve along with Tarleton's legion.

Having arrayed the inexperienced Virginia and North Carolina militias on the left and center, respectively, and de Kalb's veteran Delaware and 2nd Maryland Continentals on the right, Gates suddenly realized his mistake in pitting weakness against strength, and attempted to reorganize his deployment. With his adversary temporarily at a disadvantage by the shuffling of units, Cornwallis initiated a pre-emptive strike. On entering musket range, Webster's force fired a volley into the enemy militias, followed by a bayonet charge, and shouts of "Huzzah!" Fog and smoke soon obscured the battlefield, and the Virginians, having received bayonets only the day before and not being trained in their close-combat use, dissolved into the nearby woods, abandoning small arms and artillery as well as their colors.

The panic quickly spread to the American center, as Webster capitalized on his success by turning into the North Carolina militia's flank and the reserve 1st Maryland. Watching the unfolding disaster, Gates ordered de Kalb to continue fighting, before abandoning his command without notice and riding to Charlotte, some 60 miles to the northwest. De Kalb, unaware of the developing American rout because of the poor visibility brought on by gunpowder smoke, initially made progress against Rawdon, but with his Continentals increasingly isolated, and their commander soon mortally wounded, their stand quickly dissolved. Although some 800 North Carolina militiamen continued to effect an isolated stand, the prospect of 2,000 converging British Regulars forced them from the battlefield as well.

AUGUST 16, 1780

Battle of Camden

A view from the elevated ground bordering Gum Tree Swamp, looking east across the British line at Camden. Although these Longleaf Pines are relatively young, mature varieties covered much of the battlefield in 1780. (Author)

This memorial marks the spot on the battlefield where de Kalb was killed. (Author)

In the aftermath of the American defeat at Camden on August 16, 1780, Tarleton pursued the rebel remnants north to Rugeley's Mill along Grannies Quarter Creek. The undeveloped, swampy terrain surrounding the main battlefield helped the defeated rebels escape. (Benson J. Lossing, 1850)

With his victorious army dispersed and vulnerable should the enemy rally and counterattack, Cornwallis ordered Tarleton to charge ahead to settle any doubts. Harrying the Southern Army remnants north along Flat Rock Road leading from Camden into North Carolina, the exhausted legion conducted a final skirmish southwest of Grannies Quarter Creek near Rugeley's Mill. Within an hour, the entire battle was over. As part of the captured stores, the British found several pardons, indicating many of the enemy had reneged on their word not to take up arms against the king. Those captured with them in their possession were publicly executed, while the remainder was to be sent to confinement in Charleston.

Some 10 miles distant, Marion's group had been awakened by the distant gunfire from Rugeley's Mill, which he believed to be Sumter returning to the main army, but, on encountering a British detachment instead, he quickly set off for Witherspoon's Ferry (now called Venters Landing).

THE PLAN

Having attempted to support the Lower South and confronting what appeared to be a determined British and Loyalist effort to secure the region, and to salvage at least some of their colonial interests in the Americas, Washington's efforts against Cornwallis in South Carolina had failed. As any further attempt to field a conventional force faced the law of diminishing returns, the American commander-in-chief worried that those men and material that could be accumulated would have to content with a humid, disease-ridden climate and a minimally developed transportation network, and might not possess the endurance to remain in the field until the expected French military and financial support arrived. Should this force prove insufficient to the task, rebel militias were not seen as a viable alternative because of their loose military bearing and limited strength. For the best guarantee of success, Washington focused on leadership and appointed Nathanael Greene, by now a major general, to the command of the Southern Army, until the enquiry into Gates' conduct was concluded to satisfaction. Although he was confident in his appointee's martial abilities and resolve, Washington believed Greene would struggle with every disadvantage, including a dearth of military resources and inexperienced recruits, and assigned von Steuben to provide valuable organizational and training assistance as he had done for the Continental Army.

For the foreseeable future, militias represented the only organized rebel resistance in the Lower South after Camden. With South Carolina all but overrun by British and Loyalist forces, American partisan commanders in the colony would have to maintain viable commands in the field until the reconstituted conventional army could be brought into play in order to secure captured territory and draw local support. Although one or more of these partisan bands could gain enough popular support and resources to transform into a more established force, there were no adequate safe zones in South Carolina in which to accomplish it, and Cornwallis would certainly have quashed any fledgling effort. The best option for rebel militia commanders would be simply to outlast their conventional and irregular Loyalist opponents.

Following the reintroduction of conscription in 1776, all males between the ages of 16 and 60, except for government officials, minorities, or students, were pressured to receive at least some military training in their respective colonial militias. As most of these part-time civilian soldiers came from modest or poor backgrounds, were illiterate, and unaccustomed to military-style discipline, they generally signed on in return for land grants or bounties more than any sense of patriotism, although enthusiasm for the revolutionary cause was prevalent. Unlike an established army, there were no salutes, medals, inspections, drills, or parades while in partisan service. Whereas young, unattached men predominated in the Continental Army, those in the militias tended to be older, with established families and livelihoods, although teenagers and boys frequently participated. As militiamen were free to come and go as they pleased – as could their units – Marion seldom had the same people under him for more than two weeks at a time, with many returning home during the winter or switching sides as fortune dictated. With South Carolina having an average per-capita income twice that of New England, in large measure because of free labor, its citizens earned some of the highest wages in the colonies, making a return home from active service more attractive than in the north.

As distributed partisan commands typically operated with inferior numbers and resources, maintaining a rapid battlefield tempo was essential to their ability to successfully harass and demoralize their enemy via hit-and-run

COMBATANTS OF MARION'S CAMPAIGNS

Active from June 6, 1775 until its capture in Charleston on May 12, 1780, the rebel 2nd South Carolina Regiment (1) represented a well-disciplined, full-time formation of "regulars" that was versed in Steuben's "Continental" and artillery drills, as well as independent, irregular tactics. Their white-lined blue coatee had red facings, with which they wore a white linen waistcoat, split shirt, breeches, black leather cap, gaiters, and whitened buff-leather belts. The soldier presented here sports a bayonet in a leather frog, and a 10.5lb, 61^7/$_8$in-long English Long Land Pattern 1756 musket (third-generation Long Land Brown Bess) that fired a 10mm ball.

The British 63rd Regiment of Foot (2), aka the "Green Horse" regiment, so named for the color of their uniform facings, served in the American Revolutionary War between 1775 and 1781, often under Banastre Tarleton as a supplementary mounted infantry element. While British grenadiers and "battalion" companies respectively wore bearskin hats and tricorns, members of the

regiment's light company donned a modified civilian black worsted wool felt hat, with a cockade, loop, and button. This light-company soldier wears a red coatee and white linen or wool gaiter-trousers, and is equipped with a standard black leather cartridge pouch. A white linen haversack, kidney-shaped tin canteen, and a painted canvas knapsack would also be carried. He wields a 7lb, 43.5in English Rifle Pattern 1776.

Clean-shaven in accordance with Marion's desire to maintain hygiene and promote discipline, fighters under his command (3) wore a variety of civilian frontier clothing that was suited to the rigors of campaigning in South Carolina's backcountry. As well as military accouterments from previous service, or those gained during campaigning, this guerrilla wears a white cockade affixed to his tricorn, denoting his service with Marion's force. He possesses a canteen, powder horn, hatchet, leather cartridge box, cloth satchel, bed roll, leather belt stained brown, and carries a 6.2lb, 43.5in frontier carbine.

attacks on logistics or similar soft targets of opportunity. Successful insurgent groups relied on a leader who understood their limitations and abilities, and who knew how best to employ their often fluctuating numbers. The exploitation of formidable terrain that limited the maneuver of conventional forces was a potent way in which lightly armed and mobile militias offset their relative weaknesses in technology, organization, and numbers. The region's swamps and forests also provided potentially safe zones in which irregular forces could take refuge, rest, and reorganize, and bases from which to maintain or expand the struggle.

As a guerrilla leader, Marion was tasked with organizing insurgent structures from among the local population and establishing the moral superiority of his cause as part of the larger rebellion. This provided a critical means of sustaining the struggle because – along with maintaining positive contact with the people for whom they were fighting – it blended cultural and social causes with a political end, and served to differentiate the rebel effort from that of their enemies; a necessary approach, albeit contrary to that to which an aggressive command was accustomed. While the insurgents had already begun the process of supplanting state functions, and spread a persuasive message, absolute popular support could never be guaranteed. To maintain the guerrillas' battlefield validity, however, Marion needed to garner and maintain as much support as possible to ensure acceptable logistics, recruiting, and security. Reliable intelligence was also important, either from the protected public or defectors, as insurgents survived by remaining elusive.

In addition to securing – or denying – industrial assets such as grist (grinding grain/plant dyes, e.g. indigo), lumber, loom (textile), and iron or metal-shaping mills, the guerrillas sought to deny their enemies any sanctuaries or options for external support and attacked their opponents ideologically by exploiting religious, cultural, and political beliefs. Each side's cultural and political behavior, conventions of victory or defeat, and rules of engagement were based on unique historical and social experiences, which needed to be understood to maximize efficiency most effectively and command and control. While most tried to demonize an irregular enemy, the local population generally had a more nuanced view, and often sympathy, which also needed to be accommodated. With much of the anti-British sentiment in the Carolina backcountry stemming from an animosity to the religious authority wielded by the Anglican Church, Presbyterians and other religious "dissenters" were viewed with disapproval, aversion, and discrimination. As Marion's area of operations contained a majority of these immigrant descendants, harnessing revolutionary fervor was seldom an issue, and those initially standing neutral were often pushed toward the rebel camp as a result of the overly aggressive, and sometimes justifiable, actions of some British commanders, although the use of terror to intimidate the population was seldom beneficial to either side's long-term military or political goals.

As was typical of such encounters, the established British authorities tended to rely on urban areas or military bases from which to maintain logistics for their forces in the field, and control captured territory. While they frequently used force to eliminate the rebellion in the south, numbers alone would not

suffice. In such cases, an indirect approach often presented a better solution, as it emphasized advising, equipping, and supporting Loyalist groups. With the rebellion having grown primarily from the surrounding rural areas, Marion knew that military success translated into increasing support, from which a broader guerrilla campaign could develop. As larger areas were won over, what had originated as small, independent militias could commensurately become more established and numerous bands, contesting Crown authority on increasingly equal terms. If left unchecked, such actions would deliver to the rebels sufficient public support, territory, and communication networks to force a political settlement and end the fight. With the British "Southern Strategy" flawed – in that it was predicated on broad Loyalist support to largely supplement the effort – those disorganized rebel forces remaining in the field between the fall of Charleston and the British victory at Camden were given enough breathing space in which to regroup.

The British government was more stable than that established by the colonies via the Articles of Confederation drawn up by the First Continental Congress in mid-1776. The former also had seemingly inexhaustible resources when compared with those of the fledgling colonial resistance, although the great distances involved meant it often took the British several months to transfer men and material to the theater. British military forces also possessed greater combat experience and superior numbers, and enjoyed the support of the world's largest navy. Many soldiers were mercenaries and lacked the motivation of those fighting to defend their land and gain independence, while British officers were aristocrats who bought their rank and were often simply seeking adventure.

A brocaded silk vest purportedly owned by Marion. During the pre-industrial colonial period, all clothing was hand tailored and sewn, generally by men. Equipment and weapons were similarly handcrafted by leather artificers, blacksmiths, gunsmiths, coopers, and the like. (Author, courtesy of the Berkeley Museum)

Weapons of the period. From top: British dragoon pistol (made by R. Warkin Pistols), triangular-section bayonet, sword and scabbard, "RP" button, and British smoothbore carbine. These items were captured at Kings Mountain on October 7, 1780. (Author, courtesy Kings Mountain NPS)

Cornwallis, like most commanders, yearned for a conventional fight, and became focused on gaining contact with and defeating a conventional rebel force, rather than continuing to consolidate his gains in South Carolina. Unwilling to be baited into a fight the guerrillas could not win, Marion was committed to avoiding such a scenario, while attacking the enemy's logistics and their advanced and isolated posts that were spread throughout the interior. Given sufficient time and space, a relatively small guerrilla contingent could remain a viable fighting force. Time represented the most important element in successfully conducting an insurgent campaign, as it could be used to compensate for deficiencies or weakness, and steadily drain an adversary's resolve. Space offered freedom of maneuver and the ability to determine where, when, and whether to fight. If their adversaries appeared in overwhelming numbers, irregulars could simply withdraw and fight when the odds or chances were in their favor. As the British needed to defend large sections of South Carolina, inferior rebel militias compensated by massing to achieve localized tactical superiority and success.

With such a small force, Marion was forced to adopt an operationally defensive stance, in which costly pitched battles were to be avoided as he undertook tactical offensives to harass and stretch enemy resources further. Upon its success, attacks against the enemy's physical and moral strength would work toward a stalemate that would neutralize the Crown's presence in rural areas. Although traditional battlefield tactics emphasized linear formations and massed-volley fire, the generally restricted, rugged wilderness of the Carolinas made such fighting impractical. European cavalry simply did not work in the rugged terrain of America; of the 24 British cavalry regiments in existence, just two were used in the colonies. When mounted elements were employed, it was generally for pursuit, communication, and reconnaissance. The horse was a primary asset to a partisan command, and it was often difficult to get the men off their mounts to engage on foot, which was necessary when fighting in rugged or close terrain. Marion preferred to have his command conduct charges while on horseback, but to dismount to use small arms. The artillery used in America had to be smaller than the pieces in Europe in order to negotiate the terrain over great distances.

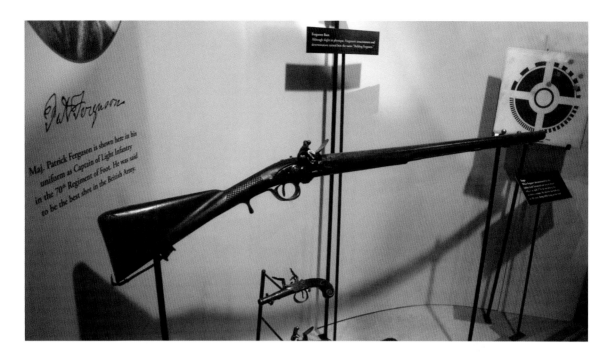

Understanding that assaults during darkness or at dawn imparted the greatest degree of surprise, Marion regularly trained his men in the essentials of partisan fighting, not only to keep them sharp for combat, but also to provide something productive to do during periods of inactivity. A proponent of active, sometimes aggressive reconnaissance, Marion went so far as to use scouts positioned in trees, and to employ distinctive whistles that could be heard over a considerable distance. As a security measure, he almost never notified his subordinates of a raid's objective or expected duration and, when encamped for any length of time, he had all water transport in the immediate area destroyed except his own. When British forces burned patriots' houses, Marion was also known to order the shooting of enemy pickets in retaliation – an unethical practice according to prevailing military convention.

Marion's men were outfitted with a variety of weapons and equipment. Only officers possessed swords, usually of poor quality, while the remainder tended to use hatchets or similar bladed weapons. Marion's men used their own weapons, generally shotguns, "firelocks," and hunting rifles, although pistols were uncommon, and field-artillery pieces almost non-existent. Captured firearms, such as the ubiquitous "Brown Bess" musket, were also employed. His command tended to use multiple-pellet loads (buckshot) for their smoothbore weapons because there was always the chance of hitting more than one man with a single discharge, especially at close range, and, when rifles were available, militias pioneered accurate, aimed shooting – something not stressed in contemporary military manuals. Bullets were cast of pewter, often collected from households, and on occasion Marion's men had as few as three rounds each. As such, they commonly had to obtain more from captured stores, or from casualties, while bayonets were used in combat infrequently, being "better for roasting a fowl."

With only 100 examples produced, the .615-caliber Ferguson rifle was an early breech-loading piece, where a turning trigger guard dropped a breech plug to permit loading. Accurate to an impressive 250yd, it could be loaded and fired while the user remained in position. (Author, courtesy of Kings Mountain NPS)

THE RAID

Although the American Southern Army in South Carolina had been routed at Camden, rebel partisans remained at large, including Sumter's 800 militiamen and Continentals. The guerrillas were temporarily protected by being on the Wateree River's west side, but the British would not be kept away for long owing to the Wateree's numerous ferries, private boats, and fords. As Cornwallis idled at Rugeley's Mill and awaited Tarleton's return from scouring the American remnants from the battlefield, word arrived of Sumter's capture of the British supply convoy from Ninety Six, some 90 miles to the west. Wanting to regain the wagons, and eliminate the possibility of the rebels' dissolving into numerous guerrilla bands that would disperse his forces and hamper his communication and logistic routes with Charleston, he ordered Major Patrick Ferguson's elements of the 71st Regiment of Foot and Lieutenant-Colonel George Turnbull's Loyalists from their positions to the west and north respectively, to block Sumter's route toward North Carolina. Although his men were exhausted by the previous night's march and the ensuing action, Tarleton also set off in pursuit early the next morning with a 350-man contingent of his legion and light infantry from the 71st Regiment.

Just south of Camden, detachments from Sumter's command succeeded in capturing a redoubt guarding a crossing over the Wateree River. Being burdened by 108 prisoners – Loyalists and Regulars from the 71st Regiment – plus 68 supply wagons, 300 head of cattle, and a flock of sheep, however, the aggressive, imaginative, and often recklessly brave rebel leader made unexpectedly slow progress to the east bank. Recognized for an aversion to authority, Sumter was known to quarrel with subordinates, and reward his men with slaves and Loyalist booty, practices collectively called "Sumter's Law." Other militia commanders simply advertised that anyone who joined would be similarly compensated, something Marion was against – although he would make an exception for horses and food.

The day after the American rout, Marion, Peter Horry, and about a dozen partisans arrived at Witherspoon's Ferry late in the afternoon. Awaiting

them at the important Lynches Creek crossing were several hundred able-bodied men and boys from Kingstree, Berkeley County (Captain William Dukes), and Lower Craven County (Captain Henry Mouzon), idling with their personal mounts, muskets, and fowling guns (shotguns) of various calibers, as part of the James Militia Battalion. Most of the interrelated and clannish volunteers had no tents or baggage, but recent events had made them all anxious to seek retribution. Many were unfamiliar with their new, seemingly uninspiring commander as he rode up to them in his coarse-textured crimson jacket and small leather helmet sporting 2nd South Carolina's silver crescent inscription of "LIBERTY." Marion likely scrutinized them in return.

Until state governments were reinstated in Georgia and South Carolina, unpaid volunteer militias offered an expedient. Most recruits had at least a modicum of home schooling or similar education, which was relatively high for the period, although they were also of little mind to conform to traditional military discipline; this potentially hampered command and control, combat effectiveness, and security. Officially a lieutenant colonel of the Continental Line on special assignment, Marion held no rank in his new command, but his seemingly hard visage and quiet reserve apparently made a positive impression. Hardy, wiry, and taciturn, he made no dramatic speech or ceremony, perhaps believing his actions would speak for him.

With sufficient provisions available on August 17 to conduct Gates' mission to cut communications between Camden and Charleston, Marion ordered his men to attach white cockades to their hats for friend-or-foe identification, as their largely civilian attire would be very similar to that of their Loyalist adversaries, who tended similarly to affix green tree sprigs. He then sent Peter Horry and four militia companies down the Santee River to destroy watercraft as far as Lenud's Ferry, recruit members, post guards at crossings, and seize arms and ammunition, for which receipts were fairly provided, although destroying privately owned boats eroded civilian support. Marion set off for Kingstree with 52 men, with a similar goal upstream.

Witherspoon's Ferry on the Lynches River was located near the road bridge shown here on the left. On August 17, 1780, Marion arrived at Witherspoon's Ferry to accept command of the Williamsburg District militia. Along with nearby Britton's Ferry, only the town of Kingston provided a route between Georgetown and North Carolina. (Author)

AUGUST 18, 1780

Raid at Fishing Creek

Clash at Fishing Creek

Having gained intelligence from recently captured Continentals, Tarleton pursued Sumter's force along the Wateree River. Although his prey's advanced guard presented an attractive target, with its 108 prisoners, 150 rescued American militiamen, and captured wagons loaded with arms, stores, and ammunition, there was no way to attack Sumter's force without becoming entangled with the main force. The dragoon commander instead crossed the river in preparation for attacking the enemy's rear contingent, while sending a mounted force to make contact with Turnbull and Ferguson and coordinate the effort. With the British infantry finding it difficult to keep up with their mounted compatriots owing to traveling over rough terrain in the high heat, Tarleton pushed ahead with 100 dragoons and 60 light infantry riding double. The remainder followed as best they could, and were to act as reinforcements should the mounted element run into trouble.

At daybreak on August 18, British scouts reported Sumter's extensive encampment at the fords near the Catawba River settlement, some 25 miles northwest of Camden. Although rebel scouts patrolled the surrounding area, they did not act as if they were anticipating trouble. With their muskets stacked, 100 Continentals and 700 militiamen passed the morning cooking, relaxing, and swimming, while their commander purportedly slept under a nearby wagon. Exploiting his unexpected opportunity around midday, Tarleton deployed his cavalry and infantry (now on foot) and charged into the enemy's midst. Although Tarleton's light infantry faltered when their captain was killed, the British quickly secured the enemy's small arms and overwhelmed the startled Americans in several skirmishes. Tarleton called a halt to the fighting only after the British and Loyalist captives were released. With the rebels having suffered 150 killed and wounded, and 350 captured, a badly wounded, half-dressed, and barefoot Sumter fled on an unsaddled horse for Charlotte. At the price of 15 casualties, Tarleton had also recovered 16 baggage wagons, a pair of 3-pdr "grasshopper" cannons, and 800 horses, which he took back to Camden and a pleased Cornwallis.

Named for its propensity to jump on firing, the British 3-pdr "grasshopper" (here a replica is shown) was a lightweight bronze cannon suitable for use in rough terrain. The water bucket was used when sponging the barrel between rounds, while the far wall holds tools including a sponge and rammer, wormer, linstock, vent pick, and tampion. (Author, courtesy of Cowpens NPS)

Marion's raid on Nelson's Ferry

With Cornwallis having been concerned that Camden was "so crowded and so sickly," and that the rebel prisoners might develop "some pestilential fever," he ordered them relocated to Charleston in clusters of 150. One escort, under Captain Jonathan Roberts, comprised 14 men from the Loyalist Prince of Wales Regiment, and 22 from the 63rd Regiment of Foot, a veteran formation that had seen considerable action since mid-1775; they took their charges south, skirting the High Hills of Santee toward Nelson's Ferry. After passing through Sumter's extensive abandoned plantation on August 19, the prisoners were marched along a bluff leading to a path crossing over the low-lying "Farrar's Savannah." Once past the swampy basin and the Santee River, they stopped for the night on an elevated, relatively dry property surrounding a nearby tavern known as the "Blue House."

Although a Loyalist deserter had notified Marion of Gates' defeat, the partisan commander said nothing to his 60-man command lest they become demoralized, and possibly dissolve as militia were apt to do in such circumstances. Receiving word from his scouts later in the day that the British had recently destroyed much of his "Pond Bluff" property, and that American prisoners were being moved along the Santee River for Charleston, Marion abandoned indirect action and rode hard for the area's only suitable crossing, some 6 miles to the east. Unlike Sumter, Marion fretted over details regarding assault preparation, reconnaissance, and coordination as he formulated a plan for his untested command.

Quietly crossing to the Santee's right bank that night, he ordered Hugh Horry to take a 16-man detachment from the Cheraws District Regiment to the ford across the swampy Horse Creek tributary to block any enemy withdrawal toward Camden. Marion led the remainder behind the "Blue House," where the oaks, cedars, and dense foliage running along a fence provided concealment. Still in good spirits from their recent victory and not anticipating further fighting, those of Roberts' command not guarding prisoners or maintaining a perimeter spent the evening eating, drinking apple brandy, and singing at the main building and adjacent arbor.

A few hours before dawn on August 20, the British and Loyalists had long since settled in for the night, with their weapons stacked nearby. As Hugh Horry's contingent emerged from their position and advanced toward the compound, a nearly full moon apparently provided just enough illumination to make them visible to a sentry, who suddenly fired on the approaching figures. Exploiting what surprise remained, the rebels rushed into the enemy camp, firing their weapons, and noisily giving the impression of a larger force. Adding to the chaos, Marion's concealed men similarly attacked from a second direction, their commander's little "cut and thrust" sword at his hip being rumored to be so rusty as to not separate from its scabbard. Roberts' group was ill prepared for an attack, with most weapons stacked on the porch and near the gate under guard. Horry left a few men to secure the weapons, but by now the British and Loyalists were suffering disproportionate losses, and their calls for quarter were accepted. Once Roberts had been pulled from his hiding place in the tavern's chimney, his men were surprised to see what a small rebel group had accomplished, for the loss of two wounded.

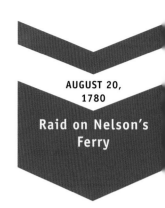

AUGUST 20, 1780

Raid on Nelson's Ferry

Overleaf:
As members of the British 63rd Regiment of Foot and a force of Loyalists escorted American prisoners captured at Camden to Charleston, Marion's newly minted guerrilla command affected a rescue early on August 20, 1780.

After the American captives were released, surprisingly only three joined Marion's command. The remaining 75 Maryland and 72 Delaware Continentals refused, whether believing the war was now lost, or viewing the ragged backwoods militia as not up to acceptable standards; 85 desired to continue to Charleston for what they assumed would be a brief detainment until the cessation of hostilities, while the remainder headed for Wilmington, North Carolina, of whom 57 ultimately arrived. Marion's men, although not dissuaded from their cause, were likely circumspect, but now sufficiently armed with captured muskets, bayonets, and ammunition, they set off for the friendly territory of Britton's Neck to avoid pursuit. Arriving the next day at Port's Ferry after a 60-mile ride, Marion ordered old saw blades rounded up from nearby iron or metal-shaping mills to be fashioned into several supplemental broadswords. With July/August and possibly September/October being harvest time, many of Marion's men desired to return to their homes to tend crops. Unlike regular formations that mandated set service terms, with no authority over his men's participation Marion consented, although he remained concerned about an enemy response. It was Cornwallis's first encounter with Marion's small force, which the British commander inflated to 150.

A reconstruction of the appearance of a private of the 2nd South Carolina Regiment, 1776. The use of the crescent derived from the English tradition in which the first-born son would receive all of his father's estate (sun), while the remainder got nothing (moon) – a reflection of the colony's self-sufficient, independent-minded citizens. Its inscription reads "LIBERTY." (Author, courtesy of Berkeley Museum)

The British response

With the Southern Continental Army's remnants filtering into the surrounding countryside or making for the relative safety of North Carolina, Marion's small force was essentially the sole rebel power still active in northeastern South Carolina. Looking to exploit his victory at Camden and crush what he saw as a resurgent rebellion, Cornwallis informed his scattered post commandants: "all of the inhabitants of this province who have subscribed, and have taken part in this revolt, should be punished with the greatest rigor; and also those who will not turn out, that they may be imprisoned and their whole property taken from them or destroyed," and "every militia man, who has borne arms with us, and afterwards joined the enemy, shall be immediately hanged!" Prominent colonial members who refused to make oaths of Crown allegiance were often exiled to St Augustine, the capital of Britain's East Florida colony.

Intent on eliminating Marion's command and subduing rebel sentiment, while demonstrating Crown authority, Cornwallis ordered Major James Wemyss to take his 63rd Regiment from the High Hills of Santee toward Kingstree, swing north to the Pee Dee River, and return via the predominantly Welsh-settled "Cheraws" ("Cheraw Hills"). Although he was aware of the strong rebel sentiment in the Pee Dee River area, and seemingly in spite of the inconsistent Loyalist support in the vicinity, Cornwallis felt that the Loyalists could be employed to secure the river's ferries and bridges and provide active patrolling. With his logistics secured, he reasoned he could move into North Carolina, where his army's presence would draw

At Nelson's Ferry on August 20, 1780, Marion conducted his first raid as commander of the Williamsburg District militia, in which he freed some 150 Continentals, captured four days previously at Camden. The area surrounding that stretch of the Santee River has since been flooded to create South Carolina's largest reservoir, Lake Marion. (Author)

further Loyalist support. As many of Wemyss' men remained sick from the region's stifling climate and disease, Major Commandant John Harrison's South Carolina Rangers and other mediocre provincials from Colonel Samuel Bryan's North Carolina Volunteers provided support. In addition to some of Tarleton's Legion, Cornwallis sent part of Hamilton's Royal North Carolina Regiment and around 100 militiamen to Radcliffe's Bridge across Lynches River to cover Wemyss' northern flank, as he conducted his punitive path of destruction. Of the uninspiring number that responded to his calls for Loyalist militiamen, most were of questionable quality.

Skirmish at Kingstree

A week after his successful raid at Nelson's Ferry, Marion's concerns about retaliation became a reality. On August 27, he dispatched two-dozen volunteers under Major James to gather intelligence on the size and disposition of Wemyss' command in Williamsburg District. Marion also wrote to Peter Horry to notify him finally of the American defeat at Camden and to tell him that, because Gates had relocated to Charlotte, the militia would soon have to temporarily retire to North Carolina, with as much as they could take in the form of supplies, weapons, and ammunition. Leaving 50 men to garrison the redoubt at Port's Ferry, Marion led his remaining 100 mounted militiamen across the Pee Dee and Lynches rivers to confront the emerging threat at Indiantown.

That night at Kingstree, Major James's command concealed themselves in a thicket beside the road into town, where they quietly counted one of Wemyss' detachments in the darkness of a nearly new moon. As the rearguard passed, the rebels rushed forward to take several prisoners in a brief scuffle, before returning to Marion, now about a half-mile from Major James' home, near town. Arriving to discuss the situation about an hour before dawn, their mounted commands waited nervously. Major James reported that one of the prisoners revealed that some 200 British Regulars and several Loyalists were at Kingstree, while another 200 under Wemyss

AUGUST 27, 1780

Skirmish at Kingstree

One of Marion's favorite locations for a forward operating base – in part because it was in the rebel stronghold of Britton's Neck – was Port's Ferry on the Pee Dee River. It was well positioned as a point from which to monitor and interdict enemy movement between Georgetown and inland South Carolina. (Author)

were to join them. Baggage taken from an enemy officer's orderly book provided further information on the intentions of the British, while other intelligence indicated that Major James Moncrief was already in Georgetown, preparing defenses with a 200-man garrison. As Marion expected to fight no more than 150 soldiers and had little desire to confront such odds, at the meeting's conclusion it was decided to withdraw to Port's Ferry, even though it meant abandoning family and property to a vengeful enemy.

Skirmish at Blue Savannah

In addition to Wemyss pushing through Williamsburg District, and the British presence at Georgetown, Marion received corroborated news from the young son of a rebel sympathizer on September 3 that a force of some 250 Loyalists was heading for Port's Ferry from the north, intent on attacking the next morning to catch the guerrillas "napping." Acting quickly to retain the option of withdrawing to North Carolina, Marion decided to launch a pre-emptive strike on what was likely an overconfident, largely undisciplined enemy, and maximize the impact of his own numerically inferior force. To ensure security, he kept his plan to attack the following morning to himself.

Although many of the Scotch-Irish in the Britton's Neck region supported the rebellion, some had remained loyal to the Crown. Under Major Micajah Gainey (Ganey), a former member of the 2nd South Carolina, the Little Pee Dee Company and other Loyalists had been organized from the Catfish and Downing Creek areas in the colony's northeast. Reinforced with elements of the 63rd Regiment and militia from Bladen County, just across the North Carolina border, Gainey intended to surprise his rebel adversary, and set off with a 45-man vanguard before dawn on September 4. The remainder of his force, some 80 mounted and 125 infantry militia, followed, likely under another former regiment member and competent commander, Captain Jesse Barfield (Barefield), who had left the rebel cause after being denied promotion.

SEPTEMBER 4, 1780

Marion's ambush at Blue Savannah

Never a heavy sleeper, Marion had already awakened to rouse his 72-man command, and sent Major James with 19 picked horsemen to ride ahead of the Kingstree Regiment, and a detachment from the Lower Craven County Regiment. On September 4, after two hours of movement through the early morning haze, one of Marion's scouts reported Gainey presiding over several Loyalists manning a roadblock not far ahead, atop a slight ridge just west of the Little Pee Dee River. Believing them to be the main enemy body, Marion ordered his own vanguard to attack the impediment from the northeast. Always impetuous, Major James charged forward and soon overwhelmed the

"General Marion in camp, during the American Revolution," illustrates what was commonly a temporary encampment; as light, rapid-deployment troops, partisans needed to move frequently to avoid detection. (Charles Scribner's Sons, 1895)

BLUE SAVANNAH

SEPTEMBER 4, 1780

Following the American rout at Camden, Crown and Loyalist forces moved to leverage their military advantage in a theatre that had devolved into a civil war over the last several years, and eliminate remaining rebel guerrillas – in particular those under Francis Marion. In response to being caught between the British garrison at Georgetown and converging Loyalist forces from Kingstree, and the Pee Dee River basin, the rebel commander initiated a pre-emptive strike from his wilderness encampment at Port's Ferry against the northern threat to preserve a route to the relative safety of North Carolina.

After surprising and defeating a Loyalist roadblock under Micajah Gainey, Marion moved to exploit his success, but having discovered the enemy's numerically superior main force, decided subterfuge was more prudent. Feigning a retreat, he instead orchestrated an ambush that defeated and dispersed his overconfident adversary. Although only a minor tactical victory, this result ensured that Marion's command remained intact; as one of the few remaining rebel forces in South Carolina it would serve as a rallying entity against Loyalist excesses, and help to strengthen rebel numbers and resolve over the next two years.

REBEL FORCES 1

1 Marion's main body

LOYALIST FORCES 1 - 3

1 Vanguard

2 Rallying Loyalists

3 Main force

EVENTS

A As a 45-man Loyalist vanguard blockaded the road some 15 miles northeast of Port's Ferry in anticipation of Marion, the guerrilla commander sent a small party in a counterclockwise movement that caught the defenders by surprise; the Loyalist quickly suffered 30 casualties.

B In response to Gainey's flight north following his vanguard's defeat, Major James offered chase, only to stumble upon rallying Loyalists. Forced to disengage as his men had not caught up, the guerrilla officer shouted orders as if he were accompanied, which scattered the already jittery group of Loyalists.

C Having continued ahead to contest Gainey's main force, Marion found his command outnumbered and instead feigned retreat, deployed into ambush positions in the thick foliage lining the road's eastern edge, and routed the unsuspecting enemy as they offered pursuit.

undisciplined enemy contingent, killing and wounding 30, and getting wounded in the process. Sighting Gainey fleeing northward with what remained of his roadblock, Major James offered pursuit. Closing to nearly sword range, the rebel commander was forced to disengage after a half-mile when he encountered several Loyalists who had rallied. Realizing his men had not kept pace and that he was alone, Major James resorted to shouting orders from behind a thicket as if he were actually accompanied. With the ruse having worked, the few Loyalists mounted up and set off into the woods or the adjacent Back Swamp.

Having soon learned that the main enemy force was encamped just 3 miles to the northeast, Marion moved to engage. After a ten-minute ride, he sighted Gainey calmly forming up his command on foot for battle. Expecting a stand-up fight, the Loyalists fixed bayonets and waited. Marion knew that to attack the unexpectedly large force was unwise and, not wanting to unduly endanger his small force, he feigned fear of the enemy and withdrew. As the terrain between the main road and the adjacent swamp to the east was covered by dense thickets, stunted pine, and scrub oak, Marion designated a select group to take up ambush positions. Likely created by ancient meteorite strikes, these low-lying, elliptical savannahs, or "Carolina Bays," were numerous in the region, with Blue Savannah so named for its otherwise sandy bottom that transformed into a sticky, bluish mud when flooded.

With Barfield arriving on the scene with little apparent thought of security, Marion's men rushed the startled Loyalists with shouts, small-arms fire, and drawn swords. Some of the Loyalists delivered fire, but as they were disorganized and attacked from two directions, firing was done individually. Although bravery played a role in the rebel success, the coolness and presence of mind of the rebel commanders and the discipline and resolve of the men resulted in a relatively cheap victory. Although the Loyalists wounded three rebels, without the protection of friendly mounted troops Gainey's command soon broke for Back Swamp. Marion followed, but with the area impassable to horses and satisfied with the results, he returned to Port's Ferry.

Back in camp the next day, Marion learned that Gainey's force had subsequently dispersed and that the Loyalist stronghold east of the Pee Dee River had been crippled for the immediate future. In the wake of such success, another 60 volunteers joined Marion's band. Should the enemy regain his strength and determination Marion had a small redoubt of musket-ball-proof logs and clay constructed on the river's east bank, backed by two small rusty field pieces, more for intimidation than for any defensive capability. The reinforced camp would also serve as an operating base from which to hamper enemy communications and logistics between Charleston and Georgetown, and Cornwallis.

On September 8, Marion's scouts revealed that Wemyss had crossed Lynches River and was approaching the rebel encampment. Combined with the nearby Georgetown garrison moving west and Gainey apparently trying to reconstitute his recently defeated force, the substantial number of troops the British deployed indicated they were attempting to encircle the rebel command. Marion and his officers held a council to determine their response. With defeat not an option lest the rebel effort in northeastern South Carolina cease, it was decided that

Opposite:
To protect what was essentially the sole rebel force in the field following the American defeat at Camden, Marion temporarily relocated to the Great White Marsh in North Carolina. Having stayed for two weeks at what was likely a rebel sympathizer's plantation, the militia commander resumed operations on September 24, 1780. (Author)

Marion would take 60 men to North Carolina and disband the remainder, to allow the men to return to their traumatized – likely homeless – families.

Marion destroyed his camp's redoubt and dragged his two artillery pieces with him as his band rode for North Carolina. Unnecessarily encumbered by the small cannon, he ordered them spiked after crossing the Little Pee Dee River, and vowed to maintain as light a force as was permissible from then on. Having ridden 40 miles, Marion's command stopped at Ami's Mill on Downing Creek. Before crossing the border, Marion remained concerned about what damage Wemyss might cause, and again sent Major James and ten picked men to monitor the situation in Williamsburg District.

Aware that Brigadier General Henry Harrington's brigade of North Carolina rebel militia was nearby at Cross Creek and would afford a measure of protection, Marion set off for the Cape Fear River. While looking for volunteers along the way, after Marion reached the southern branch of the Waccamaw River rebel supporters guided his command to a location within the Great White Marsh in Bladen (Columbus) County, just across the border. Until the situation in his home territory subsided and a profitable opportunity presented itself, Marion decided to remain in the humid, insect-infested area, likely on property owned by a rebel sympathizer and not in the swamp per se. Although his men were without tents, they settled into a dreary, Spartan existence, and bided their time.

The British retaliate

In Marion's absence, Wemyss laid a swath of terror throughout Williamsburg District that included burning dozens of homes, plundering, and killing livestock not taken with them to eliminate a source of food and clothing for the area's inhabitants, although unharvested corn was often overlooked. Anything perceived as beneficial to the guerrillas was destroyed or removed, and those who offered resistance, or were suspected of supporting the rebellion, were summarily "court-martialed" and hanged. Slaves were taken for use as British labor, many of them being sent to work on defenses at Georgetown and Charleston. The Presbyterian Church at Indiantown was burned on Tarleton's orders as such structures were purported "sedition shops," and its Irish Calvinist congregation was derided as "the most adverse of all other settlers to the British government in America." During this period, Major James's house was destroyed; his wife and children would have been killed in the subsequent collapse, were it not for the help of a sympathetic Loyalist. By September 20, Wemyss' excessive actions had turned much of the population to the rebel cause, and he soon concluded that Regular units would be needed to maintain control in his wake.

After two weeks of scavenging, malaria, and monotony, Marion looked to leave an encampment that increasingly resembled a makeshift hospital and get back into action. Seemingly ignored by Gates, Marion only received news of the wider war when Harrington told him that a new army was being created at Hillsborough, North Carolina, some 50 miles from the Virginia border. Having received news from Major James of the dire situation in Williamsburg District, during the afternoon of September 24, Marion led his command out

NORTH-CAROLINA.

By the RIGHT HONOURABLE

CHARLES EARL CORNWALLIS,

Lieutenant-General of His Majefty's Forces,
&c. &c. &c.

A PROCLAMATION.

WHEREAS the Enemies of His Majefty's Go-
vernment continuing to practife every Artifice and Deceit to impofe upon
the Minds of the People, have, as induftrioufly as falfely, propagated a Belief
among the People of this Country, that the King's Army indifcriminately makes War, and
commits Ravages upon the peaceable Inhabitants, and thofe who are in Arms and open
Rebellion againft His Majefty's Authority: I think it proper, in order to remove fuch falfe
and injurious Impreffions, and to reftore as much Peace and Quiet to the Country as may
be poffible, during the Operations of War, hereby to affure the People at large, that all
thofe who come into the Pofts of His Majefty's Army under my Command, and faithfully
deliver up their Arms, and give a Military Parole to remain thenceforth peaceably at
Home, doing no Offence againft His Majefty's Government, will be protected in their
Perfons and Properties, and be paid a juft and fair Price in Gold or Silver, for whatever
they may furnifh for the Ufe of the King's Army; it being His Majefty's moft gracious
Wifh and Intention rather to reclaim His deluded Subjects to a Senfe of their Duty,
and Obedience to the Laws, by Juftice and Mercy, than by the Force and Terror of
His Arms.

GIVEN under my Hand and Seal at Head-
Quarters in CHARLOTTE-TOWN, this Twenty-feventh
Day of September, One Thoufand Seven Hundred and
Eighty, and in the Twentieth Year of His Majefty's
Reign.

CORNWALLIS.

By His Lordfhip's Command,
J. MONEY, Aid-de-Camp.

GOD SAVE THE KING.

CHARLESTOWN: Printed at WELLS's Office, No. 71, Tradd-ftreet.

Having captured a less-than-enthusiastic Charlotte, North Carolina, on September 26, 1780, Cornwallis released this previously typed broadside urging the colony's inhabitants to relinquish their arms, in return for parole and protection. (Public domain)

of the Great White Marsh and returned south, arriving at Kingston the next day to establish a camp along the Waccamaw River. Although a Loyalist regiment under Colonel James Cassells had been sent to Britton's Neck to guard against Marion's return, Cassells had been recalled to Georgetown's garrison.

Aware that his army was still not at peak efficiency, even with the material captured at Camden, and being misinformed about the degree of Crown support in North Carolina, Cornwallis decided to invade the colony on September 25, in part because he regarded it as a sanctuary that supported the insurrection in South Carolina and Georgia. Although unhappy with his subordinate's plan, Clinton moved to send an expedition to Chesapeake Bay in order to create a "powerful diversion" and strike at the supply depots that would support Continental units sent against Cornwallis's forces. Setting out from Camden in mid-September, Cornwallis pushed north for Charlotte with four regiments of British Army Regulars, three regiments of Royal Provincials and Loyalist militia, and a cavalry detachment.

SEPTEMBER 28, 1780

Marion defeats Ball at Black Mingo

Skirmish at Black Mingo

Although Cornwallis warned that the Loyalist units of captains John Ball and Joseph Wigfall were not to be sent east of the Santee River, Moncrief believed that the small force was sufficient, and moved them north of the Black River to maintain control in Williamsburg District. As a garrison, Wigfall and 50 Loyalists took up positions near Black River Church, while Ball's 47-man command moved to Shepherd's Ferry on Black Mingo Creek to pitch camp near the "Red House," a tavern kept by the locally respected Patrick Dollard. Ball could thus control traffic on the post road, while remaining within striking distance of Indiantown and Kingstree. As an advance outpost for the recently completed defenses at Georgetown, it would help secure the primary supply point for Williamsburg District, and the British outposts along the Santee and Pee Dee rivers. Trenches were also dug along the Black Mingo, with men posted to control water traffic.

With newly arrived volunteers informing Marion of Ball's location, the rebel commander moved past Port's Ferry on September 28, crossed the Pee Dee River in flatboats, and continued to Witherspoon's Ferry, where the guerrillas crossed at dusk, and joined Captain James's contingent. Marion considered waiting for reinforcements but his command, mostly from the Lower Craven County Regiment, lobbied to attack immediately; Marion agreed and the force set off on a 12-mile ride through the night. Shortly before midnight they slipped across the boggy causeway leading to Willtown Bridge, but the noise their mounts' hooves made on the wavering planks alerted one of Ball's sentries, who fired an alarm.

Marion's men responded by quickly rushing forward and, some 300yd from Shepherd's Ferry, he ordered most of his men to dismount to fight. He reasoned that infantry would be best if Ball had fortified the nearby "Red House," and ordered Captain Thomas Waites and several officers without commands to demonstrate before the house and, if possible, initiate a frontal assault against it. On the right, Colonel Hugh Horry led a dismounted detachment from the Kingstree Regiment in a drive on the "Red House," while those still mounted were to strike on the left. Marion waited with a small reserve just to the rear.

On September 28, 1780, Marion defeated Loyalist commander Captain John Ball at Shepherd's Ferry on Black Mingo Creek. The crossing provided access between Georgetown and points north, and was adjacent to the road leading to Kingstree. (Author)

Having roused his men, Ball led them into the field near the swamp west of the "Red House," where they waited nervously as they heard Marion's approach. Ball tried to calm his command by ordering them to wait for his order to fire. With Hugh Horry's men soon emerging onto the field as shadowy figures just 30yd away, he gave the word; several rebels were quickly struck with musket fire, and the remainder staggered back but did not break, as Captain James managed to steady them. With Mouzon wounded, Captain James attempted to coordinate that command as well; he ordered Mouzon's men forward, and to remain as concealed as much as possible. Nearby, Waites pushed toward the Loyalist right, and Ball's men wavered from the two-pronged assault. After scattered firing, they broke for the relative safety of Black Mingo Swamp.

In the aftermath, Marion's men resupplied themselves with captured muskets, ammunition, and baggage. The rebels also captured nearly all the enemy's horses, with their commander taking Ball's abandoned, spirited steed, renaming it after its former owner, who soon left active service. Although their commander was intent on dispersing the 50 Loyalists at Black River Church, many of Marion's men were anxious to check on their families; Marion asked that they return to him as soon as possible. Leaving the wounded at the "Red House," Marion set off for Britton's Ferry, riding for another 26 miles before halting. Crossing the Pee Dee the next morning, he continued with the remainder of his command to Ami's Mill, where the band would remain for more than a week. While there, he delivered six recently captured Loyalists, and three from the 63rd Regiment taken the previous month at Nelson's Ferry, to Bladen County's militia commander, Colonel Thomas Brown. The Regulars had already been paroled, but, being sickly, had remained with Marion, who refrained from granting such status to the Loyalists as five had decided to join his cause; it would have subjected them to prison or execution should the British subsequently recapture them.

The British authorities were greatly concerned by exaggerated reports of Marion's strength, such as Wemyss' telling Cornwallis that the rebel commander had some 400 soldiers and growing, and his allegedly being complicit in much of the region's widespread terrorist acts and atrocities. The *South Carolina Gazette and American Journal* reinforced these views, and attempted to discount Marion's popularity by stating that he controlled his men only by the "most despotic and cruel tyranny." Because of such rumors, many Loyalists moved to Georgia or to the relative safety of the swamps, and Marion was said to have even considered moving on Charleston to rescue rebel prisoners held at Haddrell's Point. With much of his army still sick, including himself, Cornwallis worried about his now exposed flank being subject to attack from the "over the mountain men," and soon issued an express order for Wemyss to return to Camden, leaving Harrison's 80-man command in the Cheraw Hills. Major Robert Fraser was sent to aid in forming the militia, his command made up of 80 mounted men, a number of whom were combat veterans; their mission was to sweep rebel forces from between the Pee Dee River and Cross Creek. Hearing of the increased rebel activity, Cornwallis had Harrison join Fraser, and ordered all convalescents in Camden to assist.

On October 7, 1780, rebel militia surrounded and defeated a Loyalist force at Kings Mountain. This view from behind rebel lines looking up the north face shows where the British commander, Major Patrick Ferguson, fell mortally wounded. His grave is located just down the hill; he is buried with one of his mistresses, who was also killed while tending to the wounded. (Author, courtesy of Kings Mountain NPS)

As Wemyss pushed through the "Cheraws," Colonel Robert Gray arrived to replace his predecessor, who had resigned his commission in the Loyalist regiment and moved to the relative safety of Georgia. Volunteers from along the Little Pee Dee River were in short supply, however, as many were reluctant to leave their homes vulnerable to retaliatory rebel militias. The civil war in the low country, with the rice and indigo farmland running some 50 miles inland from the Atlantic coast, had become very fluid, and British efforts to conduct an established strategy were subsequently degraded; rebel bands frequently dissolved before Wemyss, only to reappear to harass him later. Maintaining communication between Charleston and Cornwallis via Camden further hampered British logistics, as men and material needed to be transported along the Cooper River to Moncks Corner, by land to the Santee River near Nelson's Ferry, and finally to the Santee and Wateree rivers, and their destination. With Loyalist attachment to the Crown fading in this region, many distressed commanders now talked about fighting a second rebellion.

In recognition of his string of successes, on September 30, Rutledge promoted Marion to colonel of the 2nd South Carolina Regiment. While he received regular reports on the enemy's activities, Marion looked to increase his force from 60 to 100 for a possible assault on Georgetown, although its defenses had been strengthened by a larger garrison, two howitzers, and an offshore galley. The governor also tasked Marion with combating groups of freed slaves working or fighting alongside the British, and to execute any suspected of carrying provisions or gathering intelligence for the enemy "agreeable to the laws of this State." Marion's force was now some 200 strong, with the recent inclusion of Colonel Hugh Giles's command, and the British now saw him as a serious threat. Cornwallis continued to profess that the Loyalists suffered from timidity and, having little sympathy or patience for their suffering, felt that if they were unable to protect

OCTOBER 7, 1780

Loyalists defeated at Kings Mountain

themselves when they held numerical superiority that there was little the British could do for them; instead, he focused upon securing the various mills in the area to supplement supply and deny them to the rebels. To make up for the shipment of horses that had been lost at sea several months previously, mounted British units commandeered horses from Loyalists which, although receipts were provided for compensation, hampered the latter's ability to conduct effective partisan operations.

While covering Cornwallis's left flank as the British theater commander reinforced his Charlotte position and plotted further movements northward, Ferguson's Loyalists were surrounded and defeated by rebel militias at Kings Mountain, South Carolina, on October 7. Essentially isolated by the loss and by continuing rebel activity against his communications and logistic chain, Cornwallis found that his position in North Carolina had become increasingly untenable. Having neglected maintaining better contact with the coast and a strong Royal Navy presence, the British general's command waited uneasily for word of their next move.

Marion's raid on Georgetown

Having recently relocated to a rebel sympathizer's property at Grime's plantation, Marion woke his men early on October 8 and rode 65 miles to Georgetown by noon. Stopping 2 miles short of the town, he scouted his objective to get an accurate idea of the defenses awaiting him. The following day he sent a 30-man vanguard ahead under Peter Horry to Georgetown's north end to draw the enemy garrison's attention, while the remainder of Marion's force wheeled around to attack the redoubt from a second direction. En route, Peter Horry clashed with Gainey's Loyalists before driving them back toward the town. During the subsequent pursuit, a man of Peter Horry's (one of the three who had joined Marion after Nelson's Ferry) thrust his bayonet into the Loyalist leader; the blade separated from the guerrilla's gun as Gainey remained in the saddle while his horse entered the town. Eventually recovering from the wound, Gainey found that his desire for fighting had been satiated, and he eventually defected from the British cause.

A reconstruction of the appearance of a member of the British Legion ("Tarleton's Legion"), a formation created in 1778 from Pennsylvania, New Jersey, and New York dragoon units, wearing the standard green light-infantry coat, black collar and cuffs, and buckskin breeches. (Author, courtesy of Cowpens NPS)

Meanwhile, Marion entered Georgetown without opposition, but found roughly 70 Loyalists taking shelter near the central brick jailhouse. Finding the nearby redoubt too formidable, Marion demanded their surrender but was curtly rejected by the commander, Colonel Cassells. After an attempt to bait the garrison from its position also failed, and word arrived that enemy reinforcements crossing the Santee River were en route, Marion paraded his men through the town, collected six of the garrison's horses and some baggage, and paroled several Loyalists. Not wanting to be cornered against the coast, Marion led his command over the Black River and headed for the swamps along the Little Pee Dee near the North Carolina border.

On October 11, Gates set up a harassing action and ordered Harrington, the North Carolina militia commander, to move from Cross Creek to threaten Gray and Fraser in the Cheraw Hills. Gates sent a dispatch to Marion congratulating him on his efforts and directing the guerrilla leader to continue to compel the enemy to disperse to deal with him. Marion was also to work with Harrington, and subsequently moved his command to the old Port's Ferry campsite; from there he called for additional militiamen, but with much of the area rebuilding after Wemyss' campaign, few responded. Fuming at the local reluctance to fight, Marion threatened to go to North Carolina to seek a command with Gates' Southern Army instead. As word got out, volunteers trickled in, and their commander decided to remain.

Until his command reached an acceptable strength, however, Marion contented himself with planning future operations, and maintaining active intelligence on localized enemy activities by sending five- to ten-man scout groups out each night, which returned in the morning. The next day, the North Carolina Board of War, apparently with Gates' approval, ordered Harrington to take control of all South Carolina militias. Unimpressed by the new appointee's military skills, and desiring to maintain his essentially independent command, Marion professed that Gates' previous order, as a Continental Army officer, trumped Harrington's authority as a militia commander.

OCTOBER 14, 1780

Cornwallis abandons Charlotte

With his left flank having been shattered at Kings Mountain, Cornwallis vacated Charlotte on October 14 and headed south over flooded streams and muddy roads. Looking for suitable winter quarters, he stopped at Winnsboro, South Carolina, to sit out an uneasy time. Realizing that Washington-style stand-up battles were simply not effective against the British in the south, the Continental Congress decided to replace Gates with the Quaker-turned-military commander, Major General Nathanael Greene. Attempting to salvage his tarnished reputation, Gates went south to try to retrieve the situation, telling Washington that he was "… going to fight a partisan war in small bands …" and would "… attack the British outpost in wilderness."

On October 24, a rider from Williamsburg District informed Marion that Wemyss had been ordered back to Camden with his mounted detachment of the 63rd Regiment, and that Lieutenant Colonel Nisbet Balfour – the Charleston commandant, and one of Cornwallis's most trusted officers – had directed Colonel Samuel Tynes, commander of the Loyalist militia of the High Hills of Santee, to turn out the militia from along the Black River. At Camden they had drawn muskets, ammunition, blankets, and saddles, and had marched to Tearcoat (aka Tarcoat or Tarcote) Swamp, where they bivouacked.

In response, Marion set off from his camp near Waccamaw with some 150 men to contest the enemy movement. As was his fashion, he told no one of his true plan, although, as his command crossed Port's Ferry for Kingstree, he indicated the goal was to attack Major Commandant John Harrison's Loyalists at McCallum's Ferry on Lynches River. Passing through Kingstree early the next day, Marion led his men for Salem and, after sunset, turned off the road and forded the Black River. As he approached Tearcoat Creek he sent a couple of boys ahead to scout the enemy encampment, who reported that Tynes' men held a strong position along the road with Tearcoat

Swamp behind them. Unaware of the impending threat, but maintaining a security perimeter, the Loyalists passed the time playing cards and music, and relaxing. Not far off, Marion rested his men until midnight.

Skirmish at Tearcoat Swamp

Early on October 26, Marion organized his force into three groups with the strongest in the center, a tactic he used successfully at Black Mingo. Once in position, he signaled the attack by firing his pistol and his men surged forward with shouts and musket fire. During the fight, Marion's bodyguards from Williamsburg District remained at his side. With each brother over 6ft tall, John, Samuel, Robert, and Lemuel Nesmith provided excellent shooting skills and an intimidating presence throughout many of their commander's actions.

The startled enemy could not organize an effective defense and many, including Tynes, fled for Tearcoat Swamp. Those who were able fired some haphazard shots at the swarming rebel shadows before withdrawing to avoid being ridden down. Having inflicted 20 casualties in a short amount of time, at the expense of two horses killed, Marion called off the fight. In addition to the rebels capturing 80 horses, a similar number of muskets, and several blankets, many Loyalists switched sides. Tyne had escaped, as had Ball at Black Mingo, and Marion was hoping that, if the enemy's leadership could be eliminated from the conflict, their followers might be more inclined to defect. In response, Marion sent Captain William Snipes into the High Hills to bring in Tynes and other Loyalist officers before Marion led his men back to Kingstree. Soon after, Snipes soon returned with his quarry.

Marion was now strong enough to deploy patrols ranging along the roads, which forced the Crown's supply wagons from Charleston to Camden to detour along lengthier routes. The British were outraged by Marion's ability to run roughshod in areas they felt were under their control, and Balfour sent 50 men to Moncks Corner to act as a buffer against the rebel commander crossing the Santee River and moving on Charleston. Cornwallis urged the

Having been informed of a Loyalist force operating between the Black River and Wenee Creek, Marion moved north from Kingstree, where he found the enemy encampment near Tearcoat Swamp. Dividing his command into three sections, he attacked and defeated Samuel Tynes' force during the night of October 26, 1780. (Author)

Just east of Richardson's plantation, Woodyard Swamp encompassed Jack's Creek and served as a starting point for Marion and Tarleton's seven-hour, 26-mile chase that ended in Ox Swamp on November 8, 1780. On period maps the area was known as "Pine Land, the Lowest in the Province." (Author)

establishment of posts in the High Hills and at the Kingstree Bridge to preserve communications. In response, Lieutenant-Colonel George Turnbull, commanding at Camden, wrote to Tarleton at Winnsboro on November 1, urging him to bring down his British Legion and eliminate the threat to Charleston's logistics. Tarleton, just recovering from yellow fever, was eager to get back into action and, although he felt chasing partisans around was beneath him and his dragoons, he accepted the mission with Cornwallis's approval.

Marion learned of Tarleton's movements and tried to surprise him, but the dragoon commander had laid his own trap at Woodyard Swamp. Warned of the plan, Marion rode off, and a frustrated Tarleton burned some 30 plantations and houses between Jack's Creek and the High Hills, in an unsuccessful move to draw his elusive adversary into the open. As an experienced partisan commander, Turnbull estimated that the enemy comprised some 1,000 militiamen at their headquarters at Singleton's Mill. With both commanders similarly skilled in irregular tactics and reconnaissance, neither fell for the other's attempts to provoke a fight.

On November 5, having learned that Tarleton was heading south and would likely cross the Santee River at Nelson's Ferry, Marion awaited him at nearby Jack's Ferry. Intent on ambushing his adversary, the rebels planted leafy branches along the edge of Woodyard Swamp and waited for two days, before receiving news that Tarleton had eluded him and was now encamped 4 miles to the north along the Santee River. According to a local slave, Tarleton was informed that a large group had gathered at Jack's Creek.

Believing the rebel band would follow, he had led his men to the plantation of Dorcas Nelson Richardson, the widow of recently deceased rebel commander Brigadier General Richard Richardson. Tarleton then positioned two small "grasshoppers" and stationed his men in concealed positions. Spreading the rumor that he had returned to Camden, Tarleton sent out patrols to entice Marion into an ambush; he hoped to do this by "Tokens of Fear," erratic movements, and by having his decoys leave campsites with provisions still cooking over the fires. Marion sighted the campfires, assumed it was Richardson's house that was burning, and set off for the plantation, while remaining alert for enemy patrols he knew were operating nearby.

An important Santee River crossing between Camden and Charleston, Nelson's Ferry drew attention from both sides as they looked to use it, or deny it to the enemy. Sumter's plantation was just beyond the left bank. (Harper & Brothers, 1851)

Richardson's Plantation to Ox Swamp

Richardson's family operated the important ferry 20 miles downstream; sympathetic to the rebel cause, Dorcas Richardson did not want Marion to become entrapped, and so her son, Captain Richard Richardson, went quietly to warn him before dawn. A former Continental officer who had been confined to Haddrell's Point following the fall of Charleston until pardoned for having contracted smallpox, Richardson had remained in hiding ever since. Halfway to Jack's Creek, he met with Marion, whose command was creeping up to deliver a surprise attack on the dragoon camp at daybreak. Being informed by Richardson that two artillery pieces, 100 cavalry, and 300 infantry lay in wait for him, Marion wisely withdrew across country, and did not halt until his men were on the far side of Richburg's Mill Dam, 6 miles away.

That evening, one of the rebel prisoners escaped to inform Tarleton of the situation, upon which he had his "boys" torch the plantation barn and surrounding outbuildings, and loot or destroy what valuables they could not take. Although allegations that Tarleton ordered the widow to be flogged to divulge information on the rebels and her husband's remains to be exhumed cannot be proven, he did set fire to the main house, in which the family survived because of the compassion of one of Tarleton's officers. Before dawn on November 8, Tarleton set off in pursuit of the rebel militia.

On learning of the escaped prisoner, Marion correctly deduced that Tarleton would follow, and also roused his own command before dawn. Local rebel sympathizers who were familiar with the area's animal trails and paths were chosen as guides, and Major James was designated as rearguard commander. Marion then led Tarleton on a 35-mile chase to the head of Jack's Creek, Ox Swamp, and finally the Black River. With much of his flight taking

NOVEMBER 8, 1780

Marion is pursued from Richardson's Plantation to Ox Swamp

Tarleton destroyed Richardson's plantation on November 8, 1780, after using it as a headquarters. The Richardson family plot remains on the property, at the end of this oak-lined path. (Author)

With Tarleton offering pursuit from Richardson's plantation, Marion pushed through Ox Swamp (shown here just east of Manning) en route to Benbow's Ferry on November 8, 1780. (Author)

place through pine-tree woods and trackless swamps, Marion drew out the pursuit for some seven hours. At Benbow's Ferry on the Black River, Marion began to fell trees in the narrow passageway leading down to the ferry, with pickets thrown out for some distance. He then told his men that if Tarleton were to succeed in scattering them – a possibility, as Marion's men were low on ammunition – they should rendezvous farther back towards Kingstree.

When Tarleton arrived at Ox Swamp after traveling some 26 miles, however, his scouts could not find acceptable crossing routes and, even if they had, his troopers and their mounts were too weary to attempt the foreboding wastes. A frustrated Tarleton was supposed to have responded with: "Come my Boys! Let us go back, and we will find the Gamecock [Sumter], but as for this damned old fox [Marion], the Devil himself could not catch him." (As the terms "Swamp Fox" and "Gamecock" came into use only following the publication of a Marion biography some 41 years later, it subsequently became part of the myth that has grown up around the partisan commander's exploits.) Having failed to eliminate his wily adversary, Tarleton resorted on November 11 to publishing a proclamation offering pardon to "delinquents," and stated that "It is not the Wish of Britons to be cruel or to destroy, but it is now obvious to all Carolina that Trechery Perfidy & Perjury will be punished with Instant Fire & Sword." Three days later, Cornwallis recalled him.

After Tynes had been defeated, Balfour ordered Barfield to reinforce Georgetown with his mounted Tories from along the Little Pee Dee River. Barfield had recently run into Captain Maurice Murphy and led his 200 men, along with Captain James "Otterskin" Lewis, into Georgetown. With the threat of Tarleton removed, Marion looked to capture the port, which, in addition to hurting British morale, would provide his men with badly needed ammunition, salt, and clothing. Having been informed that only 50 British Regulars, mostly invalids, now made up the garrison, he moved off through Williamsburg District for the coast. Avoiding populated areas, Marion kept the plan to himself as his command set off for the one-day ride around Kingstree and over the Black River at Potato Ferry.

Skirmish at Allston's Plantation

On November 15, Marion waited 2 miles above Georgetown behind White Bay Swamp, known as the "Camp." At dawn two parties went out, with the one under Peter Horry moving across White's Bridge toward the Black River and the road leading into Georgetown. A little later, Marion received word that several Loyalists had pitched camp at Colonel William Allston's plantation, known as the "Pens," and sent Captain John Melton to investigate as well as to scout the Sampit Road leading into town; the rebel commander's nephew, Lieutenant Gabriel Marion, volunteered to go along.

At White's Plantation, Peter Horry encountered Lewis's Loyalists killing cattle, and dispersed them after a quick but violent fight. Barfield was wounded and several rebel horses were shot, including Gabriel Marion's, after which Loyalists caught him and clubbed him with their muskets. Remembering one of his assailants as having once been a guest at his uncle's house, Gabriel Marion pleaded unsuccessfully for his help. When Gabriel was recognized as being related to his famous uncle, a Loyalist mulatto named Sweat killed him with a round of buckshot that also set the victim's shirt alight. The perpetrator was captured the following day and, while he was being escorted through the swamps, one of Marion's men rode over and shot him in the head with his pistol. A furious Marion publicly reprimanded the subordinate, emphasizing abiding by the rules of war as if the guerrilla force was akin to the Regular army.

With the British position in the upcountry having become increasingly tenuous because of the Crown's defeat at Kings Mountain, the presence of rebel militias, and the threat of a resurgent American Southern Army, throughout mid-November Cornwallis employed Tarleton's force as a fire brigade. By December of 1780, Cornwallis complained to Clinton that Marion constituted a considerable problem, professing that the rebel partisans maintained their presence by terrorizing and threatening the area's population through the fear of his threats and the cruelty of his punishments. As such, the British commander had few qualms concerning Tarleton's aggressive actions, and had recently ordered Lieutenant-Colonel Thomas Browne to encourage border Indians to attack rebel settlements. Without adequate intelligence, and at the mercy of degraded supply routes from Camden and Charleston, Cornwallis's army increasingly had to live off the land.

Overleaf:
Unwilling to be baited into fighting Banastre Tarleton's forces near Richardson's plantation, on November 8, 1780, Marion led his adversary on a fruitless 26-mile chase along Jack's Creek and through Ox Swamp. To further hinder their pursuers' efforts in the low-lying, wilderness terrain, small rebel rearguards would often initiate brief ambushes or skirmishes, before remounting, and disappearing after their main force. Typically armed with flintlock pistols, carbines, and sabers, Tarleton's men wore distinctive green coats and buckskin breeches, with the officers possessing gold, instead of silver buttons.

Having crossed the Black River at Benbow's Ferry, on the border of Williamsburg District, Marion set an ambush and awaited an attack from Tarleton that never materialized. (Author)

The American army, for its part, lost most of what it had in the quartermaster's department at Camden, so that Greene faced difficulties similar to those experienced by his opponent. Over the previous four months, militias from both sides had laid waste to Greene's area of operations, having taken or destroyed almost everything of nutritional or monetary value. Greene arrived in Charlotte on December 2 and assumed command of the Southern Army. Soon after, he met with key militia commanders, including Sumter, Marion, and Pickens; not wanting to make the same mistake as Gates, Greene believed that greater coordination with militia forces was necessary to ensure military success. Skeptical of being directly subordinated to the Continental Army, the militia leaders did not entirely appreciate Greene's authority for fear of losing their respective operational independence.

Skirmish at Halfway Swamp

Having learned that up to 300 Regulars of the 64th Regiment, plus 200 new recruits destined for the 7th Regiment under Major Robert McLeroth, were escorting supply wagons to Camden, Marion looked to contest their efforts. Unlike many irregular commanders, McLeroth presented an air of honor and did not harass Williamsburg District's citizens. Marion, with several hundred men including Major James and Hugh Horry, left Snow's Island – an isolated area just downriver from Witherspoon's Ferry – and moved up the Santee Road and past Nelson's Ferry. On December 12, Marion found McLeroth on the road to Halfway Swamp; Marion divided his men into three sections before striking the British from the rear. The rest of the rebel force attacked the column from the front and flank, which drove them into an open field. The British recruits panicked, but the veterans of the 64th Regiment held firm ahead of them. The fighting took the form of a long-range rifle duel until McLeroth presented a white flag to discuss an unusual option to settle a winner; 20 of Marion's best partisans were to engage an equal number of his own to the death. Reminiscent of ancient combat in which a battle had already been decided by God, this use of "champions" was seen

as a way to minimize bloodshed. Agreeing to the contest, Marion chose Major James Vanderhorst to command a contingent of his bravest, most accurate marksmen. As the rebels approached to 100yd of their adversary, the latter suddenly shouldered arms and withdrew, accompanied by celebratory shouts of "Huzzah!" from Vanderhorst's rather confused men.

As part of a ruse to buy time, McLeroth had in the meantime sent couriers for help. One found Captain John Coffin and 140 mounted New York volunteers; Coffin did not oblige, but agreed to remain nearby at Swift Creek. That night, McLeroth built bonfires, and put on a good show to draw attention to his position before quietly slipping away and making for Singleton's Mill. Marion discovered the movement the next morning, and sent Hugh Horry and 100 partisans to intercept the slippery enemy; Horry's force soon caught up with him at the mill, but called off the pursuit when it was discovered the area had been stricken with smallpox.

The next day, Marion shut down all traffic on the Santee River and Road, which effectively halted supplies from Georgetown to South Carolina's interior; he would remain there until receiving orders from Greene to conduct intelligence for his army. As part of the ongoing propaganda war, the British *South Carolina Gazette* wrote that the "State of South Carolina no longer exists. Marion and the men who follow him are blue parties and traitors against rebellion itself, and are to be sacrificed by any regular enemy. Their violence and rapine mark their steps."

Aware that he could not win a stand-up fight against Cornwallis, Greene surprisingly divided his army, seemingly against military logic. One detachment under Brigadier-General Daniel Morgan set out on December 21 to move west of the Catawba River to raise the morale of the locals, secure supplies, and oversee the area's militia. Greene knew that if he could draw his adversary north, he could cut his logistical lifelines into South Carolina altogether. Reinforced by 1,500 men under Major-General Alexander Leslie, Cornwallis was intent on making another effort to invade North Carolina, but first he needed to make his flow of supplies more secure from the seemingly

Destroying roughly 30 rebel properties as he pursued Marion from Richardson's plantation on November 8, 1780, Tarleton finally abandoned the chase in frustration at Ox Swamp later that day. (Author)

Marion's irregulars in a typical ambush setting. Note the mix of "uniforms," and that the majority are fighting dismounted. (Wester Book Syndicate, 1899)

rampaging rebel militias. He was especially frustrated by Marion's ongoing campaign, observing that he "had so wrought the minds of the people, partly by the terror of his threats and cruelty of his punishments, and partly by the promise of plunder, that there was scarcely an inhabitant between the Santee and the Pee Dee that was not in arms against us." Incorrectly believing that Morgan's force represented a threat to his left and was en route to attack Ninety Six, the British commander responded by sending Tarleton west on January 2, 1781.

Marion was promoted to brigadier general of South Carolina Troops in August of 1780, but the act became official only when Rutledge notified the colony's delegation to the Continental Congress on December 30. With this new title now valid, the partisan commander was given control of much of the low country, which included all militias east of the Santee, Wateree, and Catawba rivers. Marion subsequently went about organizing what would be known as "Marion's Brigade," with Peter Horry and his brother Hugh commanding the mounted and foot elements respectively.

In early January of 1781, Marion's men were still attacking the British garrison at Georgetown from their Snow's Island base. With Greene gearing up for action, however, Marion dispatched 70 men to destroy the British supply bases at Wadboo, Keithfield, and Manigault's Ferry to support his superior's planned offensive against Ninety Six or Camden.

The battle of Cowpens

Having not found Morgan at Ninety Six, Tarleton pushed north to eliminate the rebel force. He had regularly achieved success by undertaking long-range, demanding rides to attack an enemy who did not expect it, but by January of 1781 several rebel commanders were getting wise to such actions, and looked to adjust their own behavior accordingly. With Tarleton catching up with his prey on January 16, near a known grazing location called the "Cowpens," Morgan had decided to stand and fight. Using the area's unique landscape and his untrained militia in his tactics, Morgan believed the overconfident dragoon commander would attack him head on. Defying military convention by placing his army between Tarleton and the Broad and Pacolet rivers, which effectively blocked any escape, Morgan hoped it would force his command to stay and fight. Selecting a low hill as the center of his position, he placed 150 North Carolina skirmishers (sharpshooters) up front, and backed them up with some 300 militiamen under Pickens; Pickens' force was instructed to fire two volleys before retiring around the left, so they could reorganize under

cover of the light dragoons under lieutenant colonels William Washington and James McCall. Anchoring the rear, Morgan positioned 550 of his veteran Delaware and Maryland Continental infantry and Virginia and Georgia militia, while the flanks were left intentionally exposed.

At 2.00am on January 17, Tarleton roused his exhausted, sleep-deprived, and insufficiently nourished men, and continued his march to Cowpens. His scouts had told him of the type of terrain in which Morgan awaited him, but Tarleton was certain of success owing to his enemy's predominantly militia force that was seemingly trapped between the mostly experienced British troops and a flooding river. As soon as Tarleton reached an appropriate location, he formed a battle line, which consisted of dragoons on his flanks, with his two "grasshopper" cannons positioned between the British Regulars and the Loyalists. Most of his infantry (including that of the legion) assembled in linear formation and moved directly upon Morgan. The right and left flanks of this line were protected by dragoon units. In reserve, Major Arthur MacArthur's 250 Scottish Highlanders of the 71st Regiment served as a veteran core, while Tarleton kept the 200-man legion contingent in reserve, ready to be unleashed when the rebels broke and ran.

At around 7.00am, Tarleton's van emerged from the woods in front of the American position, and soon went over to the offensive against a line of rebel skirmishers, who felled 15 dragoons and prompted the remainder to withdraw. To eliminate the problem, Tarleton immediately ordered an infantry charge without pausing to study the American deployment, or to allow the remainder of his infantry and his cavalry reserve to make it out of the woods. Tarleton rushed the skirmish line without stopping, and deployed the bulk of his force and two "grasshopper" cannons. The rebel skirmishers kept firing as they withdrew to join the second line manned by Pickens' militia. The British attacked again, this time reaching the militiamen, who (as ordered) poured two volleys into the enemy. The British, with upwards of 40 percent of their casualties being officers, were stymied and confused, but re-formed and continued to advance. Tarleton ordered one of his officers, Ogilvie, to charge with some dragoons into the "defeated" rebels, but as they set out they were momentarily checked by the militia's musket fire before continuing. Pickens' militia filed around the American left to the rear as planned, having fired their requisite two volleys.

A view from the Continental rear looking toward Tarleton's approaching center at Cowpens, January 17, 1781. In the war's only double envelopment, the Americans shattered the British force and achieved a decisive victory. It not only damaged the dragoon commander's reputation, but served as something of a turning point in the rebel effort to reacquire the colony. (Author, courtesy Cowpens NPS)

JANUARY 17, 1781

Tarleton defeated at Cowpens

Looking east from where Tarleton's rear pushed ahead to exploit what seemed to be an unfolding victory at Cowpens (January 17, 1781). As the British approached the enemy line, the American militia that had feigned a withdrawal turned to effect a double envelopment that caused the defeat of their exhausted, demoralized adversary. (Author)

Taking the withdrawal of the first two lines as an overall retreat, the British advanced headlong into the third and final line of disciplined Regulars awaiting them on the hill. As the 71st Regiment moved to flank the American right, the Virginia militiamen initially made to adjust their facing to meet the threat, but owing to the chaos of battle and a misunderstood order, they began to withdraw. Believing this move to be a retreat, the tired, disorganized British Regulars broke formation and surged forward to complete their anticipated victory. Morgan ordered a volley, and the Virginians responded by turning around and firing a devastating salvo from some 30yd. With the British momentarily stunned, Lieutenant Colonel John Eager Howard ordered the Continentals to conduct a bayonet charge.

Tarleton's force, faced with an increasingly intractable situation, began to collapse; some surrendered on the spot, while others ran off. Howard's men charged forward and seized the "grasshoppers," while Washington's cavalry arrived from the rebel left rear to strike the British right flank. Pickens' militia re-formed and attacked from behind the hill to complete the enemy's encirclement; this was compounded by the reappearance of rebel militia on the left flank where the exhausted British believed their own cavalry was operating, sapping what little will remained to continue the fight. Caught in a clever double envelopment, many began to surrender.

With Tarleton's right flank and center line collapsed, only a small number of the men of the 71st Regiment remained in action. Realizing the desperate seriousness of what was occurring, Tarleton rode back to his remaining intact unit. Although he ordered his legion to charge, it refused and abandoned the field, while nearby the surrounded remnants of the 71st Regiment surrendered. Desperate to save something, Tarleton managed to find about 40 cavalrymen and with them tried to save the British artillery, but they had already been captured. Tarleton, with a few remaining horsemen, rode back into the fight; he was confronted by Washington, who apparently attacked him with his

saber, calling out, "Where is now the boasting Tarleton?" Tarleton then shot his opponent's horse from under him and fled, ending the hour-long battle. The British had suffered at least 70 percent casualties in a battle in which their elite legion and dragoons were effectively destroyed; MacArthur, now a prisoner, commented that "he was an officer before Tarleton was born; that the best troops in the service were put under 'that boy' to be sacrificed." A rebel prisoner later stated that, when Cornwallis heard of the disaster, he placed his sword tip on the ground and leaned on it until the blade snapped.

With Cornwallis's position increasingly untenable, rebel partisan commanders continued to pressure British logistics and communication routes. While the British commander prepared to go after Morgan to recover the men captured at Cowpens, Marion, now with perhaps his largest force yet, continued his partisan campaign, initially joining with Lieutenant Colonel Henry Lee for another attack on Georgetown. After moving down the Pee Dee River during the night of January 22, Lee's infantry idled just outside the town to scout its now 200-man garrison. Maneuvering undetected onto the town's waterfront the following night, one party seized the garrison commander, while a second blocked enemy attempts to man their fortifications. Marion and Lee charged through the light defenses to link up with the infantry, where they were surprised that none of the British troops attempted to man the garrison. Having no equipment and wishing to avoid a costly assault, the rebel duo was soon forced to leave, however.

As Lieutenant Colonel William Washington rode forward to personally confront a defeated Tarleton at Cowpens, a British cornet (second lieutenant) from 17th Light Dragoons moved to slash the Continental commander, and was shot down by Washington's trumpeter. (Anne S.K. Brown Military Collection, Providence, RA, USA)

This view near Wyboo Swamp shows typical off-road terrain along the Santee River. It was in this area that Marion started what became the "Bridges Campaign" in March of 1781. (Author)

The "Bridges Campaign"

With Cornwallis's army in a bad way, Loyalist militia continued to fight throughout South Carolina. In March of 1781, Rawdon, the British commanding officer in Charleston, planned a two-pronged assault against Marion. Lieutenant-Colonel John Watson's 500 British Regulars of the 3rd Regiment and Loyalists from Fort Watson were to advance along the Santee River towards Marion's main force near Nelson's Ferry, "for the purpose of dispersing the plunderers that infested the eastern frontier." Colonel Welbore Ellis Doyle and the Volunteers of Ireland, in turn, set out from Camden to destroy the partisan's camp at Snow's Island.

In the first of a sequence of engagements that became known as the "Bridges Campaign," Marion and Watson clashed along the quarter-mile-long causeway over Wyboo Swamp, where the former had established an ambush, on March 6. Following several cavalry engagements on the structure, Marion was forced to withdraw when his adversary brought up a pair of cannons. Marion and Watson continued to spar at Mount Hope (March 8), Black River Bridge (March 14), Blakeley's plantation (March 15–28), and Sampit Bridge (March 20 and 28). During this last action, Watson's horse and 20 of his men were killed and he was forced to vacate the area. At the same time, Doyle destroyed Marion's base at Snow's Island (March 23), after which Hugh Horry pursued the enemy commander, forcing him back to Camden.

Final engagements

Throughout the spring and summer of 1781, Marion continued with his partisan campaign. Having rejoined Lee to hamper British logistics by capturing first Fort Watson, after a week-long siege (April 15–23), and then Fort Motte (May 12), Marion went on finally to occupy Georgetown (May 28). The two major South Carolina militia groups, Sumter's 1st Brigade and Marion's 2nd Brigade, were led by men with very different styles and operational areas, and had little need or reason to cooperate with each other – or the Continental Army, with whom, both felt, rested the primary responsibility for the fall of Charleston. After fighting several hundred dragoons and Loyalists at Parker's Ferry on August 13, Marion participated in what could be considered a true battle. On September 8, he joined Greene at Eutaw Springs, and was given command of the combined North and South Carolina militia; Marion won accolades from his superior, as well as the accompanying von Steuben.

In 1782, Marion again patrolled the area east of the Cooper River, where on August 28 at Wadboo Swamp, and the next day at Fair Lawn, he unsuccessfully attempted to ambush Major Thomas Fraser. In what was his last engagement of the war, Marion was forced to withdraw for lack of ammunition.

MARCH 6–28, 1781

The "Bridges Campaign"

ANALYSIS

As a response to the Crown's humiliating defeat at Saratoga that epitomized the military and political stalemate in the Northern Colonies, and with a recently defeated France looking for payback, the British effort to secure control of the Lower South while maintaining possession of New York proved inadequate to the task. In 1775, the entire British Army had some 48,647 men, of which 8,580 were stationed in the American colonies. The remainder was largely positioned as homeland defense against their historic adversary, France, including 15,547 and 12,533 in England and Ireland respectively. At this time Parliament believed 10,000 Regulars would be needed to suppress the rebellion. Five years later, over 30,000 soldiers were in theater, with no discernible end in sight. In May of 1780 the British had a clear numerical superiority over the rebel forces in the south, which consisted of an approximately 5,500-strong ad hoc force near Charleston. In contrast, Clinton maintained over 23,000 men in New York City, a major supply hub and symbol of Crown authority in the north that needed to be protected at all costs, as well as a fleet of some 19 warships. Even though Washington had just one-third the numbers, Clinton allocated only 37 percent of his command to the southern campaign.

Owing to the intense nature of fighting an insurgency, at the strategic level, every asset at a nation's disposal needed to be committed to ensure success. Even as the conflict in the colonies became more violent, the British were unwilling or unable to dedicate a significant portion of their military to supporting operations in North America. Unlike much of the Revolutionary War in the north, the fighting in the Carolinas was generally less civilized and more brutal, with Loyalists and rebels in roughly equal numbers. As neither the British nor their adversaries established effective civil order or protection, the region's partisan violence proved to be some of the war's most destructive and vindictive. When the British decided to open a second theater of operations in 1780, no additional forces were provided to Clinton. Operationally, Britain's North American campaign was not given top

Looking out across Lake Marion (formerly a stretch of the Santee River, until dammed in 1941) from atop Fort Watson. One of the waterway's numerous tributaries, Jack's Creek, is two miles upstream. (Author)

priority for national resources, which forced Clinton to fight with what limited men and materials were available; his failure to ensure unity of effort within the theater doomed the campaign from the start.

The British had based their counterrevolutionary "Southern Strategy" on the erroneous premise that the majority of the population in the Southern Colonies was loyal to the Crown and would provide for most of the fighting, even though ministers in London were aware of increasing evidence to the contrary. This translated into the British not allocating sufficient soldiers to ensure sustained operational success. Even though George III remained steadfastly committed to bringing the colonies back under British rule, many in Parliament, and externally among Britain's allies, advocated a cession of hostilities in order effectively to counter France. In addition to an inconsistent policy toward the Loyalists, Germain's shifting strategic priorities, and the failure to counter the threat posed by the French Navy meant that the Southern Strategy ultimately failed.

The British prosecution of their southern campaign illustrated that they lacked the necessary patience to endure a long, protracted pacification program. At the operational and tactical level, Cornwallis became quickly frustrated by the situation in the south, with its humidity and disease, guerrillas, and especially colonists, who accepted training and weapons from the British and then deserted to the enemy. His decision to invade North Carolina before completely subduing South Carolina was premature, and his desire for a stand-up, conventional fight forced him to depart from his comfort zone, rather than consolidating his gains in South Carolina, which would have forced the rebels to come to him. As rebel partisan forces focused on weak or isolated targets, the British were compelled to dissipate their strength to compensate. It was also quickly evident that many joined militias out of expediency and could not be relied upon to perform active service with the British until the latter held military ascendancy. Crown methods that were used to cripple resistance generally backfired, and served to inflame further resistance to British authority, including among those who had remained on the sidelines as neutrals.

Faced with a difficult task, Cornwallis neglected to adequately support his detachments, primarily Ferguson's and Tarleton's, defeated at Kings Mountain and Cowpens respectively; he arguably missed a chance to eliminate

Morgan after Cowpens. In addition to waiting too long before informing Clinton of his second invasion of North Carolina, Cornwallis allowed Greene time to reinforce his army. He chose to make a stand at Yorktown, when he might have informed Clinton of the inadequacy of the position before making such a final move. He also abandoned the position's outer defenses, thus depriving himself of extra time, which might have saved his army. The British, at this stage of the war, tended to be less idealistic about their cause than their enemy, and it could be argued that Washington didn't win the war, but that because of the terrain the British lost it.

A British failure to establish a civilian government after the fall of Charleston in 1780 directly influenced the outcome of the war. Official policy dictated that all of the continent was to be subdued, and only then would new civil government take form, something that likely led to the lower-than-expected Loyalist turnout. The Loyalists had become smarter over the course of the Revolutionary War, realizing that by proclaiming their allegiance to the Crown they would become targets for the Whigs. With no civilian infrastructure, and an army frequently on the move, the British were unable to provide the necessary support to their civilian allies; they tended to view their adversaries as inferior soldiers, and never fully developed the resources they had in America. Treating the war as one of conquest, rather than relying more on diplomatic measures, only promoted the deep divisions between Loyalist and rebel, and steadily eroded Crown authority after 1780; it eventually forced the cessation of operations following the loss of support at home.

For all his espoused 19th-century treatises on conventional forces, the military theorist Clausewitz largely saw the use of guerrillas as being just another resource in which the Regular army operated. Less-inhibited practitioners envisioned them in broader terms. A century later, Thomas E. Lawrence ("Lawrence of Arabia") saw that irregular forces "granted mobility, security (via denying assets to the enemy), time, and doctrine" and that "Those undertaking insurgency and terrorism are trying to find a way to use their strengths, such as mobility, organization, and relative anonymity or stealth, against the weaknesses of their more powerful adversary." Bernard Fall, a noted French war correspondent during the Vietnam War, distilled this equation even further, suggesting that "when a country is being subverted, it is being out-administered, not out-fought."

A few miles up the Santee River, Fort Watson, with its 30ft-high walls, served as a British supply-chain link with Charleston, until taken by besieging Continentals and militiamen under Lee and Marion respectively, during April 15–23, 1781. It was built atop a 1,000-year-old Santee Indian ceremonial and burial site. (Author)

Situated atop a bluff of Santee River swamp some 4 miles east of Eutaw Springs, Marion's plantation was looted by both sides and subsequently burned by the British. Rebuilt after the war, the property – along with Sumter's, located upstream, and others – has since been submerged under Lake Marion. (Harper & Brothers, 1912)

While the British remained a very disciplined and effective force, which – except for Kings Mountain and Cowpens – had won every battle in the Lower South between 1780 and 1782, the continued existence of rebel militias remained a constant source of irritation and harassment, especially to insecure or isolated targets, and supply lines. This led to constant revisions of British plans, and forced Crown assets to hold down various areas of the south for extended periods, thereby forcing the dissipation and dilution of Cornwallis's primary force. It further had the effect of minimizing Loyalist support and, in particular, enlistment in British service.

Militias tended to achieve success when focusing strictly on a particular operation's goal – unless offered a lucrative target in the process that did not unnecessarily place the group at risk – while avoiding more traditional stand-up fights. Taken individually, these southern skirmishes amounted to little, but, as a whole, rebel successes hampered Cornwallis's efforts to conquer the Lower South – an important consideration as of the war's 1,546-odd battles and skirmishes, the majority occurred in South Carolina. Irregular activities in this region caused considerable losses among the British and weakened their resolve. Furthermore, the rebels could defend in depth and maintain a flow of men from Virginia, and, until the British could control this colony, they would not be able to secure the Lower South.

What made all the difference, however, were those special individuals who understood their men's strengths and weaknesses. Commanders such as Greene were able to harness the people's will to the detriment of the British cause. The British especially hated Marion and made repeated efforts to neutralize his force, but the militia commander's intelligence network was as effective as the British one was poor, especially with the rebel-dominated Williamsburg District being positioned between Cornwallis and the coast.

Marion seldom used his men to conduct frontal attacks, opting instead for surprise hit-and-run assaults when facing larger but unsuspecting or unprepared enemy forces. Conflict in the sparsely populated southern colonies promoted non-traditional battlefield solutions and, with Major Robert Rogers, the innovative irregular leader of the French and Indian War, having encapsulated some fundamentals of irregular warfare, established formations were soon operating under such maxims. Such ranger tactics were expanded during the Revolutionary War by men such as Colonel Daniel Morgan of "Morgan's Riflemen"; according to Burgoyne, Morgan's men were "the most famous corps of the Continental Army, all of them crack shots." In a similar vein, Marion's command, generally numbering between a few dozen and a few hundred, operated on the periphery of more established Continental elements.

ACTIONS INVOLVING FRANCIS MARION*

Date	Action	Crown	KIA	WIA	POW	%	Rebel	KIA	WIA	POW	%
Aug 16, 1780	Camden**	2,239	68	245	11	14	3,052	733	1,270	66	
Aug 20, 1780	Nelson's Ferry	36	24			67	60	0	2	0	3
Sep 4, 1780	Blue Savannah	250	30		0	12	72	0	4	0	6
Sep 28, 1780	Black Mingo	50	3	1	13	34	50	2	8	0	20
Oct 7, 1780	Kings Mountain	900	127	125	648	100	940	28	62	0	10
Oct 26, 1780	Tearcoat Swamp	200	6	14	23	22	150	26		0	17
Nov 15, 1780	Allston's Plantation	200	4	2	16	11	200	2	3	–	3
Dec 12, 1780	Halfway Swamp	300	–				700	4	6	0	1
Dec 14, 1780	Nelson's Ferry	–					–				
Jan 17, 1781	Cowpens**	1,200	60	184	600	70	1,286	11	61	0	6
Jan 24, 1781	Georgetown	357	1	–	3	1	350	1	2	–	1
Feb 15, 1781	Halfway Swamp	550	–				–				
Mar 6, 1781	Wyboo Swamp	430	3	–	0	1	250	6	12	0	7
Mar 8–9, 1781	Mount Hope	430	–		0	–	70	–	–	0	–
Mar 14–15, 1781	Black River	230	12	0	–	5	–	5	8	0	–
Mar 15–28, 1781	Blakely's Plantation	–					–				
Mar 20, 1781	Sampit Bridge	230	2		0	1	100	–		0	–
Mar 28, 1781	Sampit Bridge	230	20	38	–	25	70	1	–	0	1
Apr 3, 1781	Witherspoon's Ferry	300	9	2	16	9	70	–		0	–
Apr 15–23, 1781	Fort Watson	114	0	0	114	100	350	2	6	0	2
May 8–12, 1781	Fort Motte	148	3	–	145	100	380	–	2	0	1
May 28, 1781	Georgetown	80	1	0	50	64	400	0	0	0	0
Aug 13, 1781	Parker's Ferry	660	125	80	–	31	200	1	3	0	2
Sep 8, 1781	Eutaw Springs	2,300	85	351	430	38	2,092	251	367	74	33
Feb 25, 1782	Tidyman's Plantation	700	0	1	0	0	500	20	1	12	7
Jun 8, 1782	Bowling Green	500	–		500	100	–	1		0	–
Aug 28, 1782	Fair Lawn	160	–				–				
Aug 29, 1782	Wadboo	160	4	6	1	7	40		0	0	0

* Being predominantly skirmishes, available figures are often contradictory.
** Included for perspective (Marion did not serve at either engagement).

Marion's band attacked and captured a group of Loyalists under Gainey at Bowling Green on June 8, 1782. Gainey subsequently sued for peace at nearby Burch's Mill, effectively ending Loyalist resistance in South Carolina. (Author)

Although Washington had fought in the wilderness during the Seven Years War, he was not a practitioner of irregular warfare; in fact, he was trained in the regular school of warfare and saw the ultimate success of the Revolutionary War as being based upon victory on the battlefield in the conventional fashion, rather than by employing the loose tactics utilized by rebel irregulars. While the British employed irregular warfare to some success, it never affected the war's outcome. The rebels, in contrast, used these tactics and techniques to suppress their Loyalist adversaries, and thereby isolate the British from local support.

Rebel militias represented an important element in securing an American victory, but one that was peripheral, and not acting in isolation – even as such units became more integrated with traditional forces, and acquired a degree of legitimacy among the general public. Ultimate credit for securing an operational victory in the Lower South rested with Greene and his traditional Continental Army command. Without external support, however, the British would likely have retained a presence in the colonies, and bided their time until the renewed threat from France could be alleviated. As it happened, French sea power proved a contributing factor to American independence. The English failed to apply the 18th-century understanding of conflicts – that war was a tool of diplomacy to resolve disputes and not a blunt instrument – choosing instead to attempt the total subjugation of the colonies by military means. In bottling up Cornwallis at Yorktown, and preventing British assistance by sea, the success of the French Navy's contribution was not solely dependent upon a singular and accidental lapse by a dominant British navy; rather, it was a reflection of the decline of British sea power and the rise of Britain's historic adversary. By 1777, Britain's dominance of the Western Atlantic was in decline. If luck was involved at all, it was to the benefit of the British, allowing them to escape several potential disasters before 1781. The British also repeatedly overestimated the strength of the Loyalists and failed to protect them by establishing effective control of the American interior, a violation of the "iron rule" that people tend to support political structures that protect their lives and property. The Revolutionary War broke the existing military pattern in that no towns or fortresses provided the keys to victory, requiring that the British not only achieved battlefield victories but also occupied territory.

At the end of the siege of Yorktown (September 28 to October 19, 1781), Cornwallis surrendered to American and French forces, in what was the final major battle of the war. Brigadier Charles O'Hara is depicted here formally surrendering on behalf of Cornwallis. (Library of Congress)

CONCLUSION

Completed in 1884, the *Yorktown Monument to "The Alliance and Victory"* was the first monument authorized by the Federal government, on October 29, 1781. (Author)

Having failed to secure the Lower South, Cornwallis marched into Virginia to seize the port towns of Yorktown and Gloucester. With the arrival of the French fleet of Admiral de Grasse, Washington was able to march south from New York with a joint American and French force to attack the cornered British Army. The Americans and French marched out of Williamsburg and arrived before Yorktown on September 28, 1781, forming a semi-circle around the British entrenchments. Cornwallis mistakenly expected Clinton to provide sea-based support via the York River, which bisected his primary position and Gloucester Point. Rather than return south to the Carolinas or attempt to reach his superior on his own, within two days Cornwallis was effectively trapped, with little hope of relief.

By October 9, the besiegers had moved close enough to initiate an artillery bombardment, and five days later stormed two redoubts in front of their trenches. With the British position increasingly untenable, the defenders attempted a sortie a week later in which they managed to spike guns in two redoubts, but further movements achieved scant gains. With no relief expected and running low on artillery ammunition and food, Cornwallis succumbed to the inevitable; he marched his 6,000-man command from his Yorktown entrenchments and surrendered on October 19. Afterward, British officers were invited to dine with the victors – all except Tarleton. In 1782 Parliament called off further fighting in the Thirteen Colonies and, on December 14 that year, British forces withdrew from Charleston. On December 15, Marion's command was disbanded.

On the family plot at Francis' brother Gabriel's Belle Isle plantation, Francis Marion's wife, Mary, is buried next to his tomb, which was erected in 1893 to replace the crumbling original. (Author)

On February 3, 1783 the Treaty of Paris formalized an official cessation of hostilities, and with it American independence had been achieved. Prior to the British departing the colonies the next day, some 80,000 Loyalists (over 9,000 of whom were from South Carolina) had already left the fledgling nation for Britain or its other colonial possessions to escape retribution, in one of history's largest mass migrations. Many Loyalists, however, remained, while others returned from exile to resume residence in South Carolina.

After the war's end, Marion needed to borrow money to rebuild his burned and looted home, and restock it with slaves, having served in the militia without pay. The state government achieved mixed results from its attempt to aid its depleted treasury and punish former Crown supporters by confiscating their property. Although some revenue was realized, over time many were simply forced to pay a fine. During a stint in the South Carolina Provincial Congress, Marion supported leniency toward the defeated Loyalists, and vigorously opposed the confiscation of their property. Unlike the treatment of Loyalists in the north, where they were forced to relocate to other British territories, such as Canada, Marion's tolerant actions allowed many to remain in their South Carolina homes. When the legislation offered him the same protection against lawsuits stemming from the war, unlike Sumter, Marion refused, believing that if he had "wronged any man, I am willing to make him restitution. If, in a single instance, in the course of my command, I have done that which I cannot fully justify, justice requires that I should suffer for it." By the end of the 1780s a degree of reconciliation had taken place between Loyalist residents and the state and its citizens. Of South Carolina's remaining population, up to 40 percent of whites left for other colonies and western territories. The British presence had, however, resulted in freedom for thousands of black slaves, who were taken to locations like the Bahamas and Jamaica.

In 1786 Marion married his wealthy cousin and adjoining property owner, Mary Esther Videau, and four years later voted for a federal union at the Constitutional Convention. Childless, he subsequently retired to his rebuilt "Pond Bluff" property, where he died in 1795, with a tomb inscription ending with "… lived without fear, and died without reproach."

BIBLIOGRAPHY

Babits, Lawrence E., *A Devil of a Whipping: The Battle of Cowpens*, Chapel Hill, NC, University of North Carolina Press (2000)

Borgeson, Benjamin, *The Principles of Destruction in Irregular Warfare: Theory and Practice*, Published online at http://smallwars.org/jrnl/art/the-principles-of-destruction-in-irregular-warfare-theory-and-practice - _ftn74#_ftn74 (accessed February 20, 2013)

Gordon, John W., *South Carolina and the American Revolution*, Chapel Hill, NC, University of South Carolina Press (2007)

Gruber, Ira, "Britain's Southern Strategy," in W. Robert Higgins, ed., *The Revolutionary War in the South: Power, Conflict, and Leadership*, Durham, NC, Duke University Press (1979), pp. 205–238

Hibbert, Christopher, *Redcoats and Rebels: The American Revolution Through British Eyes*, New York, NY, W.W. Norton & Co. (2002)

Horry, Brigadier General Peter, *The Life of Gen. Francis Marion*, Philadelphia, PA, Joseph Allen (1852)

Kalyvas, Stathis N., *The Logic of Violence in Civil War*, Cambridge, Cambridge University Press (2006)

Lamb, Roger, ed., Dan N. Hagist, *A British Soldier's Story: Roger Lamb's Narrative of the American Revolution*, Baraboo, WI, Ballindalloch Press (2004, first published 1811)

McLaurin III, Hugh M., *The Swamp Fox*, Dallas, TX, Taylor Publishing (1988)

Moore, Horatio Newton, *The Life and Times of General Francis Marion*, Memphis, TN, General Books (2009)

O'Kelley, Patrick, *Nothing but Blood and Slaughter: The Revolutionary War in the Carolinas, Vol. 1: 1771–1779*, Bradenton, FL, BookLocker.com (2004)

O'Kelley, Patrick, *Nothing but Blood and Slaughter: The Revolutionary War in the Carolinas, Vol. 2: 1780*, Bradenton, FL, BookLocker.com (2004)

O'Kelley, Patrick, *Nothing but Blood and Slaughter: The Revolutionary War in the Carolinas, Vol. 3: 1781*, Bradenton, FL, BookLocker.com (2005)

O'Kelley, Patrick, *Nothing but Blood and Slaughter: The Revolutionary War in the Carolinas, Vol. 4: 1782*, Bradenton, FL, BookLocker.com (2005)

O'Kelley, Patrick, *Unwaried Patience and Fortitude: Francis Marion's Orderly Book*, Concord, MA, Infinity Publishing (2006)

Otis, James, *The Boy Spies with the Swamp Fox: The Story of General Marion and His Young Spies*, New York, NY, A.L. Burt Co. (1899)

Otis, James, *The Minute Boys of South Carolina*, Boston, MA, Dana Estes & Co. (1907)

Piecuch, Jim, *The Battle of Camden: A Documentary History*, Charleston, SC, History Press (2006)

Rankin, Hugh F., *Francis Marion: The Swamp Fox*, New York, NY, Thomas Y. Crowell Co. (1973)

Savage Jr, Henry, *River of the Carolinas: The Santee*, New York, NY, Henehart & Co. (1968)

Scotti Jr, Anthony J., *Brutal Virtue: The Myth and Reality of Banastre Tarleton*, Berwin Heights, MD, Heritage Books (2002)

Simms, W. Gilmore, *The Life of Francis Marion*, New York, NY, Geo. F. Cooledge & Brother (1844)

Stedman, C., *History of the Origin, Progress, and Termination of the American War*, 2 vols, London (1794)

Swisher, James K., *The Revolutionary War in the Southern Back Country*, Gretna, LA, Pelican Publishing (2007)

Tarleton, Banastre, *History of the Campaigns of 1780 and 1781 in the Southern Provinces of North America*, Dublin (1787)

Wilson, David K., *The Southern Strategy: Britain's Conquest of South Carolina and Georgia, 1775–1780*, Chapel Hill, NC, University of South Carolina Press (2005)

INDEX

Figures in **bold** refer to illustrations

Allston's Plantation, skirmish at 59, 73
Ami's Mill 48, 51
Ardesoif, Captain John P. 22–3
area of operations **19(map)**, 30
artillery 32, 36, **36**, 65

Balfour, Lieutenant Colonel Nisbet 54, 59
Ball, John 50–1
Barfield (Barefield), Captain Jesse 42, 47, 59
Black Mingo, skirmish at **50**, 50–1, 73
Blue Savannah, skirmish at 42–3, **44–5**, 47, 73
Bowling Green, action at 73, **74**
Bridges Campaign, the 68, **68**
British Army 8, 28, 31, 32, 69–70, 72, 74
 uniforms 13, **18**, **28–9**
British Army formations 42
 3rd Regiment of Foot 68
 63rd Regiment of Foot 25, **28–9**, 37, **38–9**, 40–1, 42, 54
 64th Regiment of Foot 62–3
 71st Regiment of Foot 34, 65, 66
British failure, causes of 69–72
Brown, Colonel Thomas 51, 59
Buford, Colonel Abraham 23–4

Camden 20, 21, 22, 34, 56, 68
 battle of **24**, **25**, 25–6, **26**, 73
Campbell, Lord William 10, 10–11
casualties 17, 36, 47, 55, 65, 68, 73
Charleston 10, 13, **13**, 15
 siege of **16**, 16–18
Charlotte 20, 21, 49, **49**, 53, 54, 62
Cheraw Hills 51–2, 54
Clinton, Lieutenant-General Henry 14–15, 16, 17, 18, 20, 49, 59, 69–70, **70**
Coffin, Captain John 63
Continental Army 8–9, 11, 14, **14**, 17–18, 40, 68
Continental Army formations
 1st Maryland 25
 2nd Maryland 25
 Cheraws District Regiment 37
 Kingstree Regiment 12, 43, 50
 Lower Craven County Regiment 43, 50
Continental Congress 9, 31, 54, 64
Cornwallis, Lieutenant-General Charles 18, 20, 24, 25, 26, 27, 32, 34, 37, 40–1, 49, 51, 52–3, 54, 55–6, 59, 63, 67, 70–1, 74, **75**, 76
Cowpens, battle of 22, 64–7, **65**, **66**, **67**, 70, 73

Doyle, Colonel Welbore Ellis 68

Ferguson, Major Patrick 18, 34, 70
final engagements 68
Fishing Creek, clash at 36
Fort Motte **21**, 68, 73
Fort Watson 68, **71**, 73
French and Indian War (aka Seven Years War) (1754–63) 8, 74

Gage, Major-General Sir Thomas 9
Gainey, Major Micajah 42, 43, 47, 53, **74**
Gates, Brigadier General Horatio 18, 20–1, 24, 25, 54
Georgetown 42, 52, 53, 59, **63**, 64, 67, 68, 73
Grannies Quarter Creek , skirmish at 26, **26**

Great Britain 7–9, 10, 14, 31, 69–70, 75
Great White Marsh **46**, 47–8, 48–9
Greene, Major General Nathanael 18, 27, 54, 62, 63–4, 68, 71, 72, 74

Halfway Swamp, skirmish at 62–3, 73
Harrington, Brigadier General Henry 48, 54
Horry, Hugh 37, 50–1, 62, 64, 68
Horry, Major Peter 18, 34–5, 35, 41, 53, 59, 64

Indiantown 22, 48
irregular warfare 4–5, 4–6, 8, 28, 30, 32–3, 71–3, 74

Jack's Ferry 56–7
James, Major John 22, 22–3, 41–2, 43, 47, 48, 57, 62

Kalb, Johann von Robais, Baron de 18, **24**, 25, **26**
Kings Mountain, action at **52**, 53, 70, 73
Kingstree, skirmish at 41–2

Lake Marion **70**
Lee, Lieutenant Colonel Henry 67, 68
Lincoln, Major General Benjamin 16, 16–17, 18
Loyalist formations 18, 20
 British Legion 22, 23–4, 25, 41, 53, 59, **60–1**, 65
 Little Pee Dee Company 42
 New York volunteers 63
 North Carolina Volunteers 41
 Prince of Wales Regiment 37
 Royal North Carolina Regiment 41
 Royal Provincials 18
 Volunteers of Ireland 68

MacArthur, Major Arthur 65, 67
McCottry, Captain William 22
McLeroth, Major Robert 62–3
Marion, Francis 5, **6**, 11, 12, **12**, 20, **31**, **43**, 77, **77**; at Charleston 16; joins de Kalb's command 21; Williamsburg District militia command 24, 34–5, **35**; and the battle of Camden 26, 73; planning and preparations 27–8, 30–3; military and political goals 30–2; security 33; raid on Nelson's Ferry 37, **38–9**, 40, **41**, 73; skirmish at Kingstree 41–2; skirmish at Blue Savannah 42–3, **44–5**, 47, 73; in the Great White Marsh **46**, 47–8, 48–9; skirmish at Black Mingo **50**, 50–1, 73; promoted to Colonel 52; raid on Georgetown 53; skirmish at Tearcoat Swamp 54–5, **55**, 55, 73; pursuit of Tarleton 55–7, **56**; Tarleton's pursuit 57–8, **58**, **60–1**, **62**, **63**; skirmish at Allston's Plantation 59, 73; skirmish at Halfway Swamp 62–3, 73; attack on Georgetown **63**, 64; promoted to brigadier general 64; assault on Georgetown 67, 73; Bridges Campaign 68, **68**; action at Bowling Green 73, **74**; final engagements 68; command disbanded 76; plantation **72**; assessment of leadership 72–3; actions involving 73
Marion, Gabriel 59
militiamen **11**, 18, 27–8, **28–9**, 72, 74

Morgan, Brigadier-General Daniel 11, 12, 13, 16, 63, 64, 64–7, 67, 73

Nelson's Ferry **57**
Nelson's Ferry, raid on 37, **38–9**, 40, **41**, 73
North Carolina 14, 18, 20, 40–1, 48, 49, 54, 70

Ox Swamp 57–8, **60–1**, 63

Parker's Ferry, action at 68, 73
partisan forces 4, 20, 27–8, 35, **43**
 appearance **11**, **28–9**, 35
 tactics 28, 30, 32–3
 weapons 33, **33**
Pee Dee River **5**, 21, 40, 41, 50, 51, 67
Pickens, Andrew 20, 64–5, 65
planning and preparations 27–32
Pond Bluff 12, 37, 77
Port's Ferry 40, 41, **42**, 42, 47, 50, 54
prisoners of war **17**, 34, 36, 37, 40, 51, 73

Rawdon, Lieutenant-Colonel Francis 21, 68
Richardson's Plantation 57, **58**
Rugeley, Major Henry 18
Rugeley's Mill 24, 26
Rutledge, John 13, 52

Santee River 12, **15**, 22, **22**, 35, 37, **68**
Saratoga, second battle of, 1777 **15**, 18
South Carolina **5**, 10–11, 12, 13, 14, 20, 27, 77
South Carolina formations 11, 13
 1st South Carolina (infantry) 11
 2nd South Carolina (infantry) 11, 13, 23, **28–9**, 40, 52
 3rd "Ranger" (cavalry) regiments 11, 41
 South Carolina Militia, 2nd Brigade 23
 uniforms 13, **28–9**, 40
Southern Strategy, British 14–15, 31, 70
Steuben, Baron Friedrich von 14, **14**, 68
Sumter, Brigadier General Thomas 18, 20, 34, 36, 68

tactics 4–6, 28, 30, 32–3, 73, 74
Tarleton, Lieutenant-Colonel Banastre 22, **23**, 23–4, 36, 59, 64
 at Camden 25, 26, **26**
 at Indiantown 22, 48
 Marion's pursuit of 55–7, **56**
 pursuit of Marion 57–8, **58**, **60–1**, **62**, **63**
 battle of Cowpens 64–7, **65**, **66**, **67**, 70
Tearcoat Swamp, skirmish at 54–5, **55**, 55, 73
Turnbull, Lieutenant-Colonel George 34, 56
Tynes, Samuel 55

Washington, George 9, 15, 17–18, 18, 27, 74, 76
Washington, William 65, 66–7, **67**
Wateree River 34
Watson, Lieutenant-Colonel John 68
weapons 32, 33, **33**
Wemyss, Major James 40–1, 41–2, 42, 47, 48, 51–2, 54
Williamsburg District action 22–4
Witherspoon's Ferry 26, 34–5, **35**, 50, 73
Woodyard Swamp 56, **56**
Wyboo Swamp 68, **68**, 73

Yorktown , siege of 71, 74, **75**, 76, **76**